SERVING THOSE WHO ARE SEVERELY DISABLED:
Devices and 'Soft' images
Designs for devices for better mobility
Stories and images for those
with severe disabilities

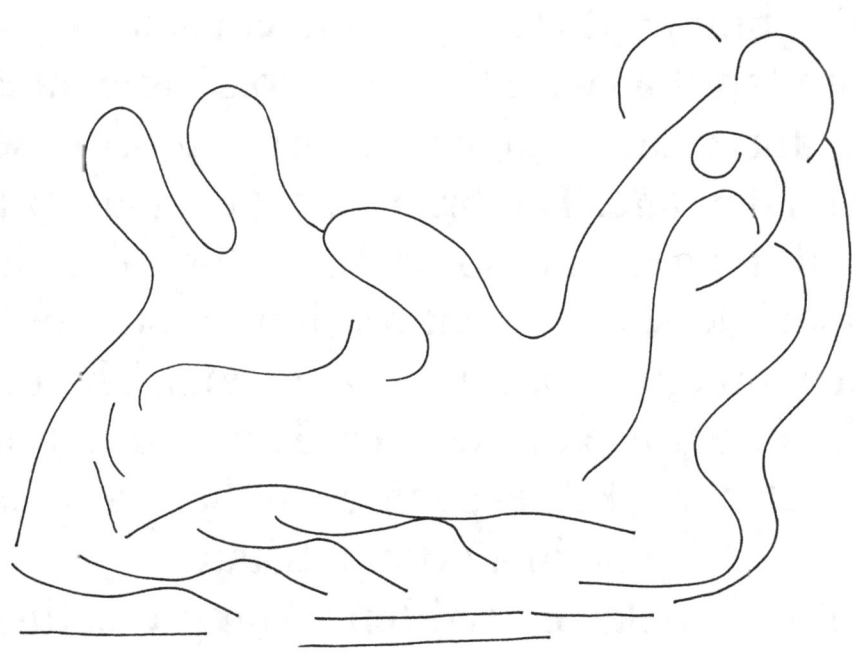

Camilia MacPherson, Ph.D., D.Th.
2016

INTRODUCTION

This book is written using Automatic Drawings.
The first section are designs for devices
that stimulate movement and healing.
The second section employs 'soft images'
in the telling of the story.
The third section uses 'soft or gentle dots'
to tell the stories.
The brain without eyes and consciousness
are familiar with the 'soft dots' language.
These stories and images are written for those with
severe brain damage. The brain has the capacity to absorb
millions of images. It is sometimes able to tap into Pure
Consciousness, a concept foreign to the intelligent
conscious mind, but familiar to Savants. The brain can
also SEE without use of the eyes. These 'dot' images and
stories can also awaken capacities in the brain that appear
to be in a dormant state.
Most of my books are written using pre-calligraphy
graphics as seen in the diagram below. There is no top or
bottom of the page. Each page has several images, and
has to be viewed from every angle and depth. The line at
the bottom of most pages are from the scanner. It serves
only as a platform.

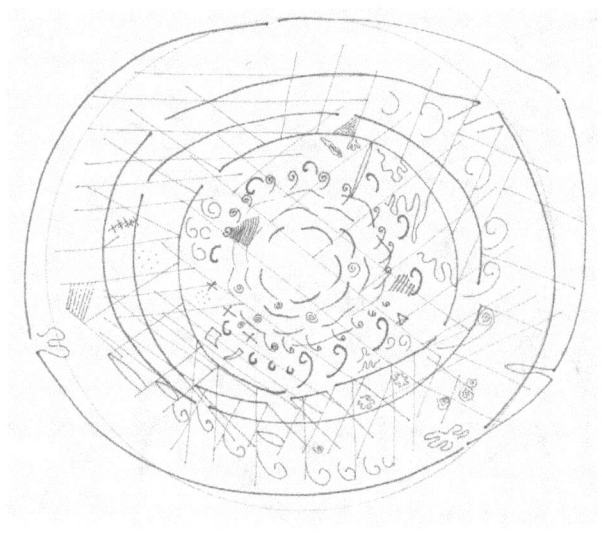

ISBN-13:978-1530708444
ISBN-10:1530708443
Email: tamaracpublishers@icloud.com

DESIGNS FOR DEVICES FOR BETTER MOBILITY AND HEALING

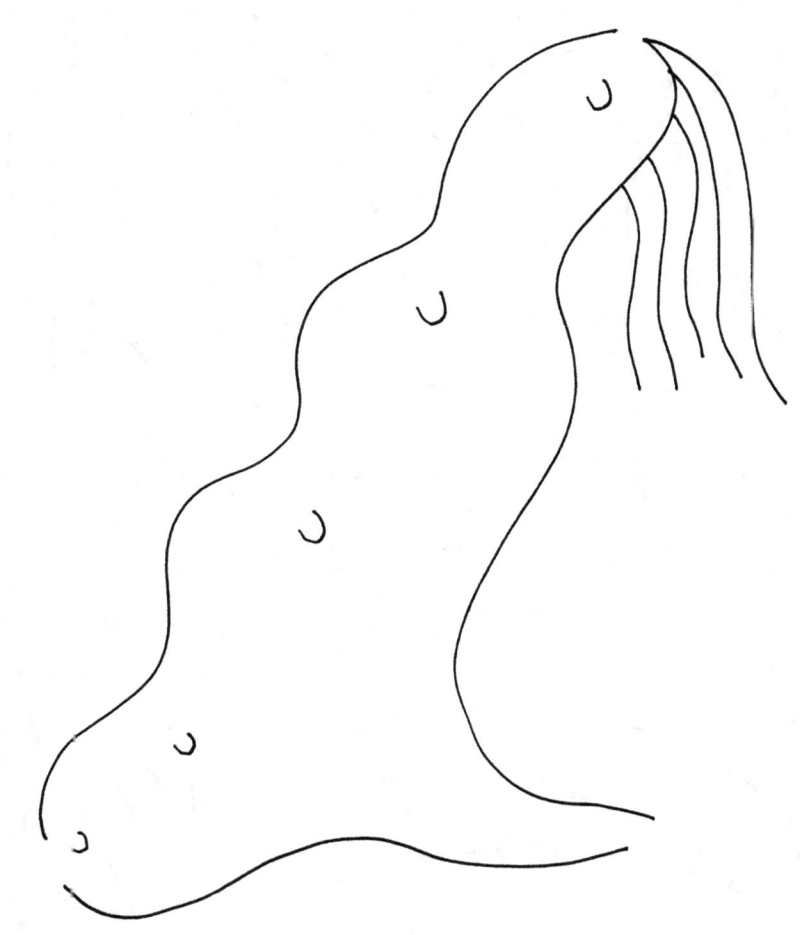

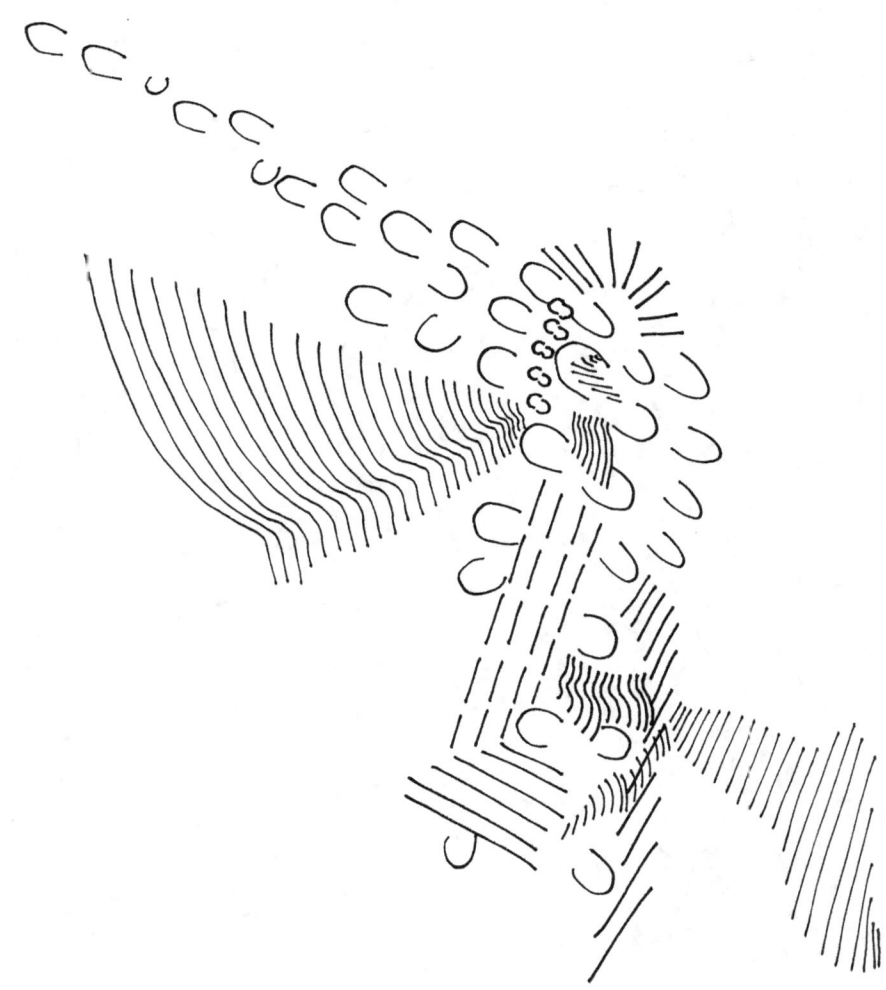

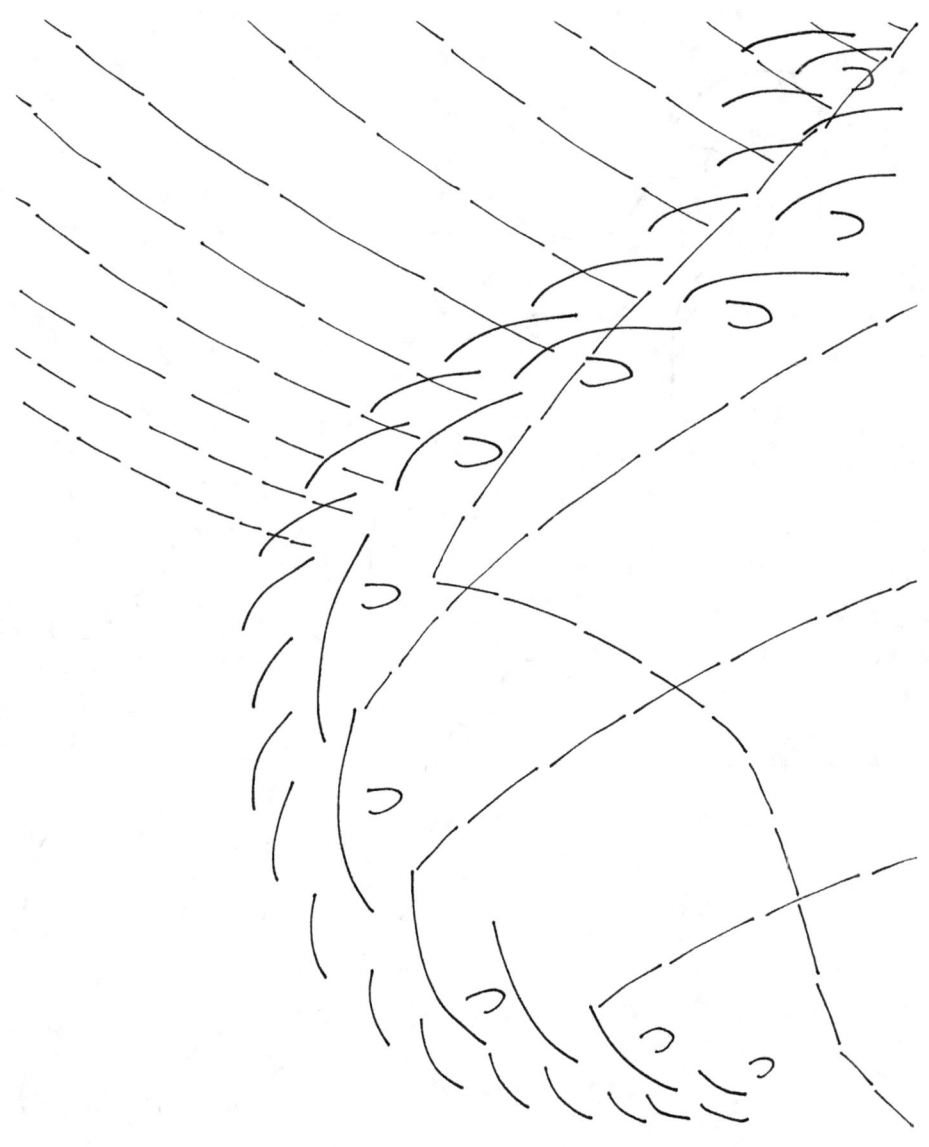

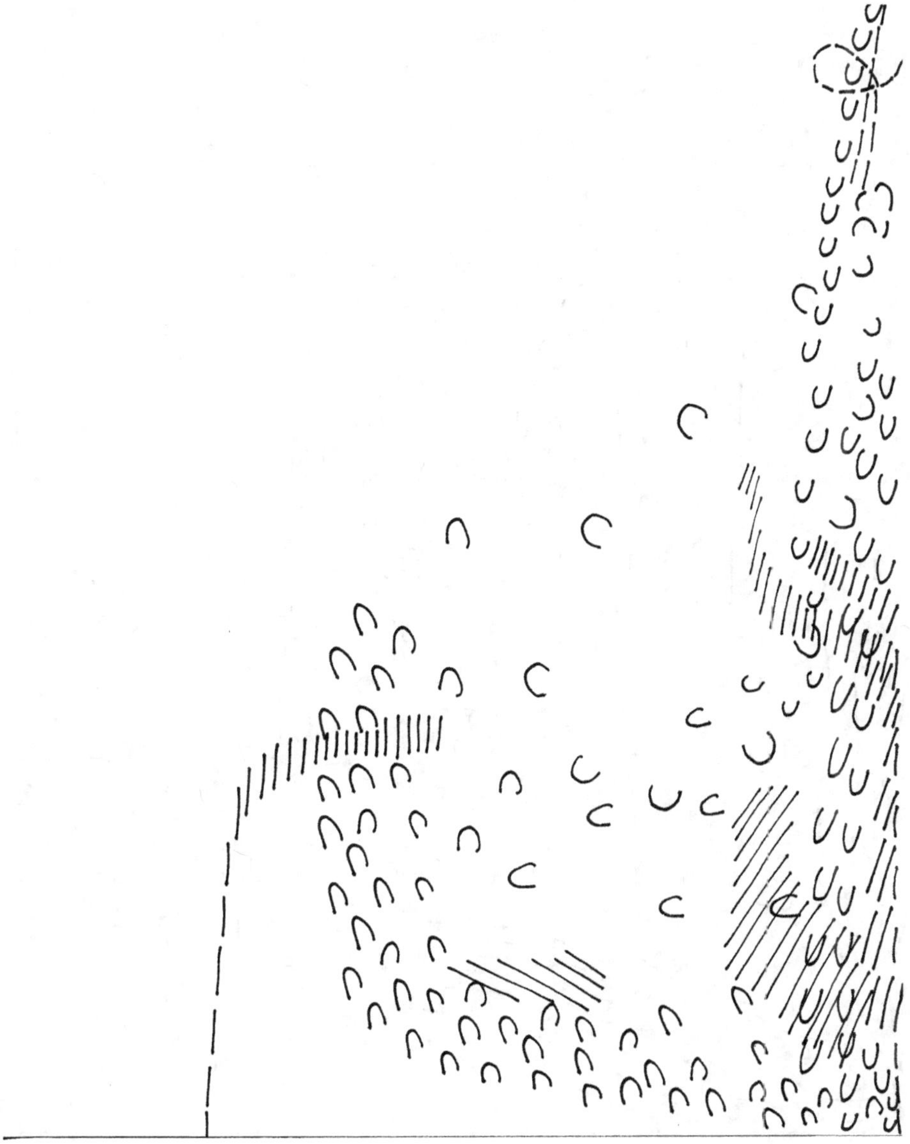

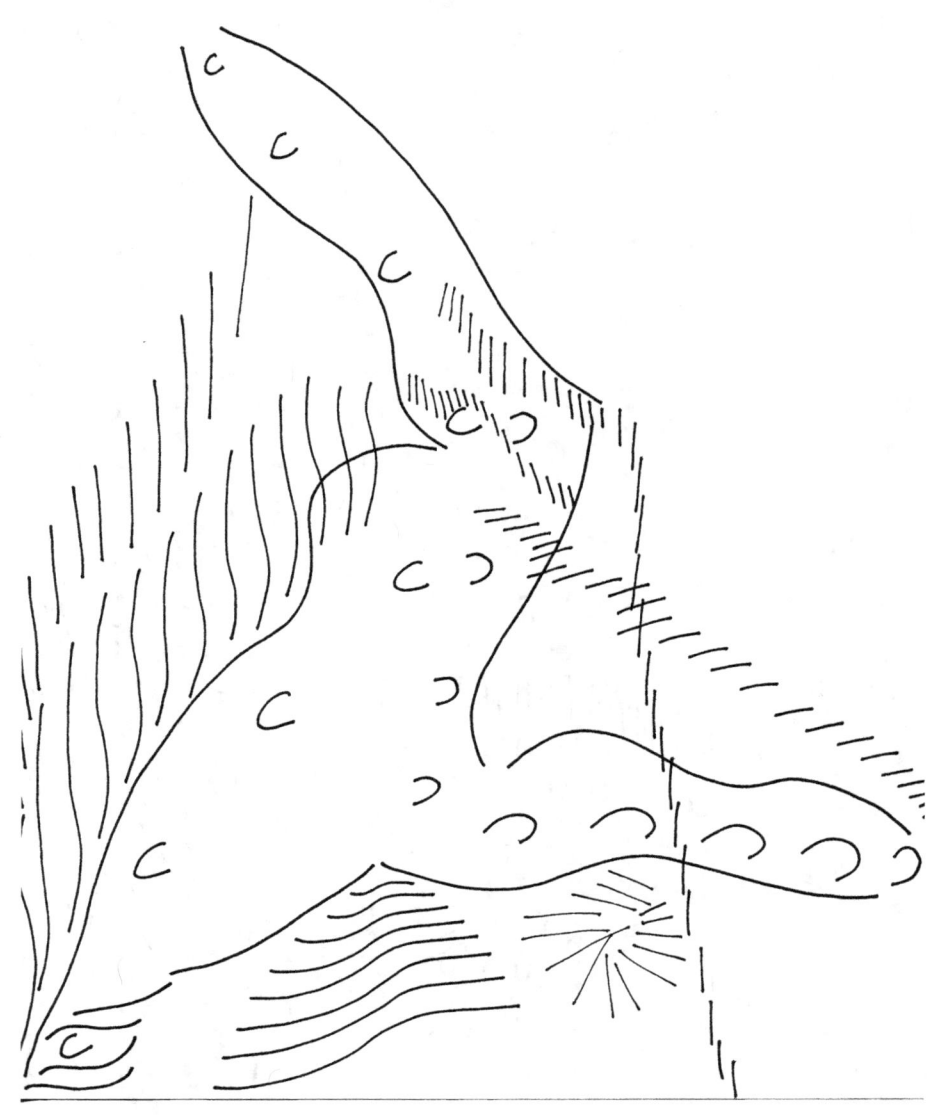

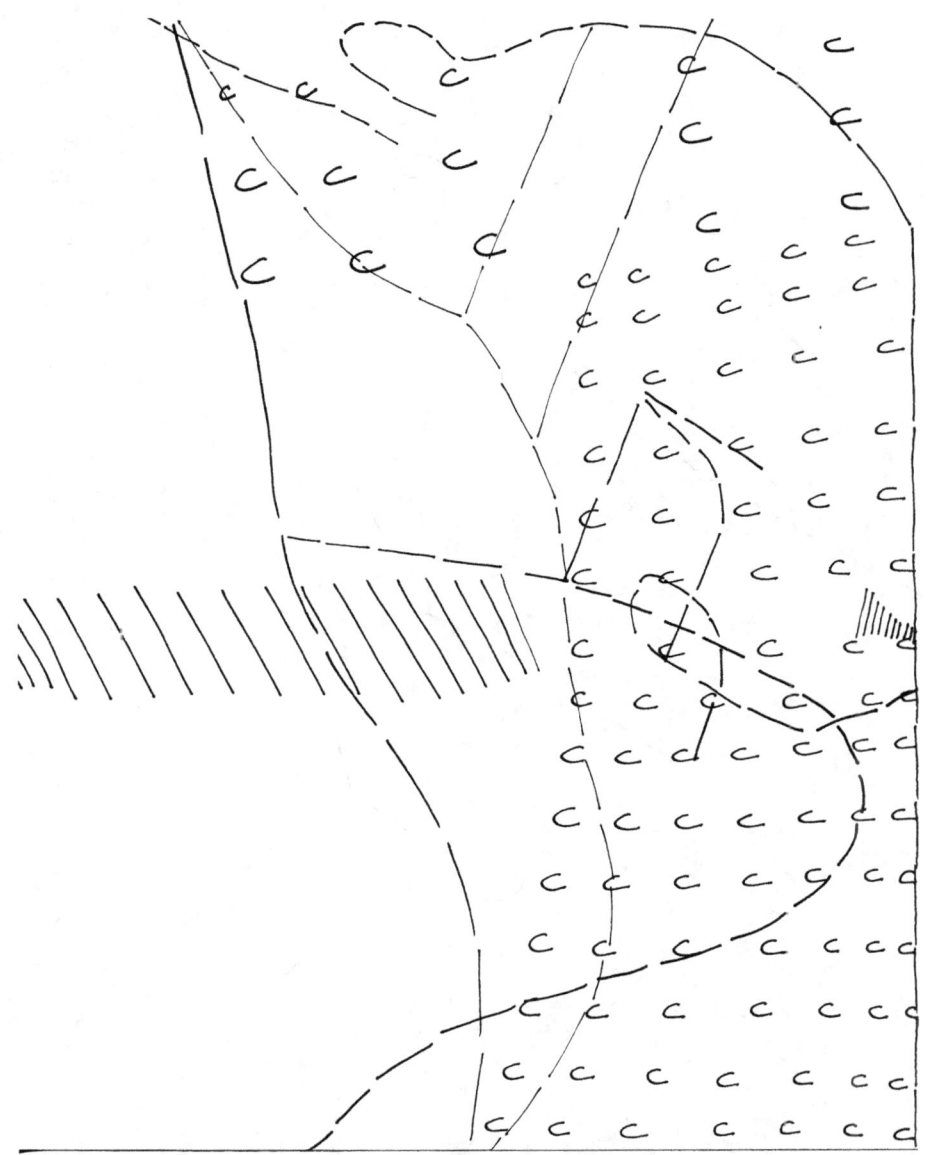

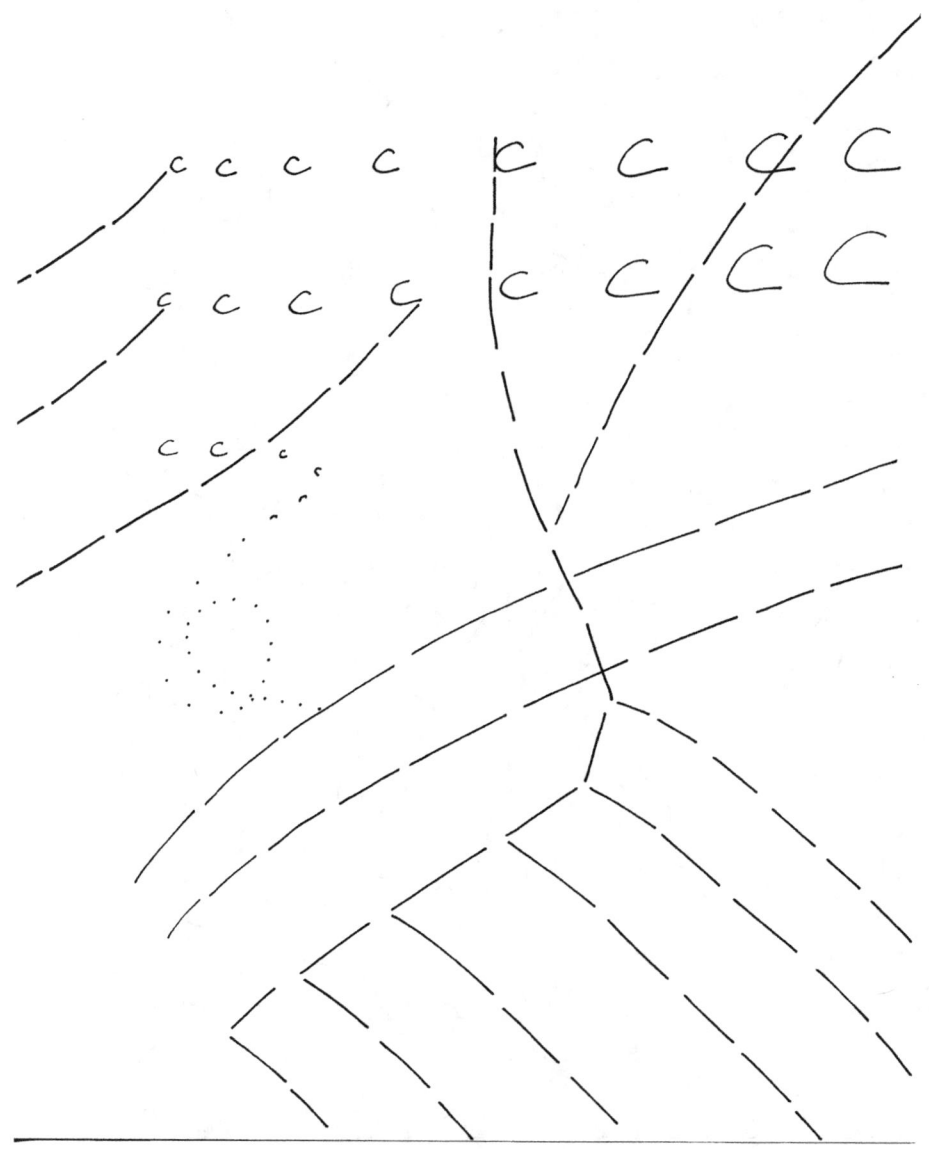

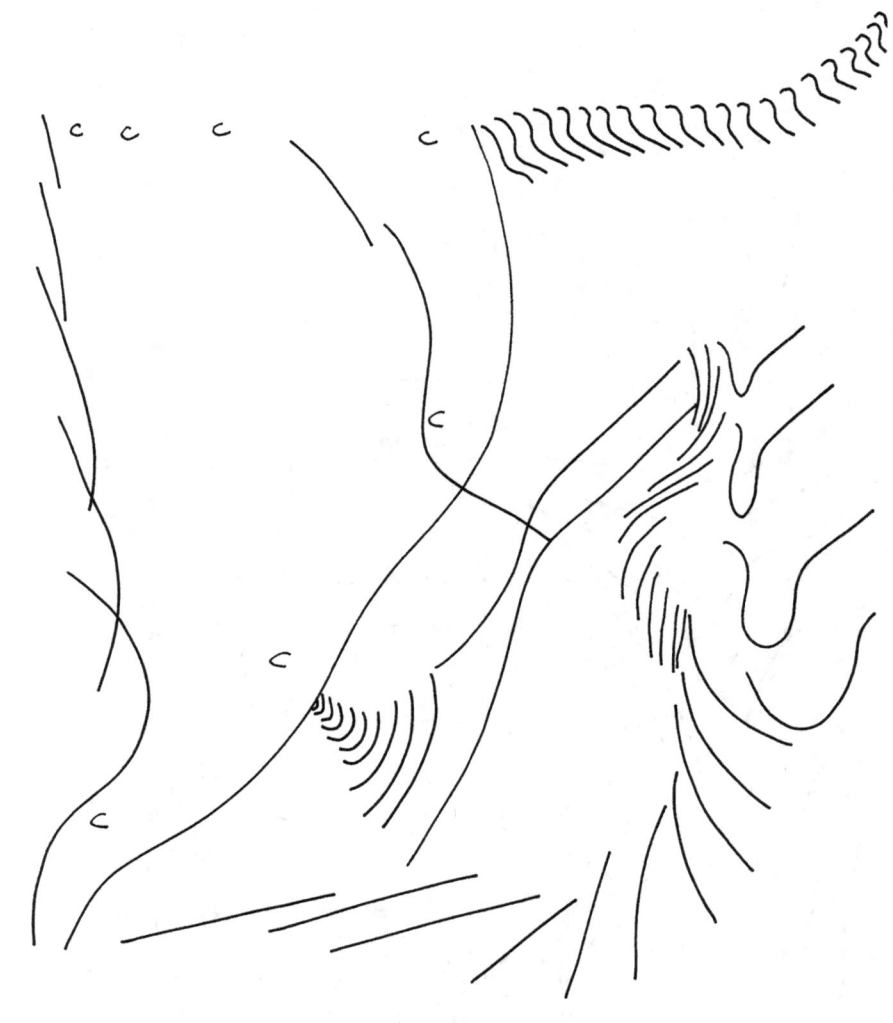

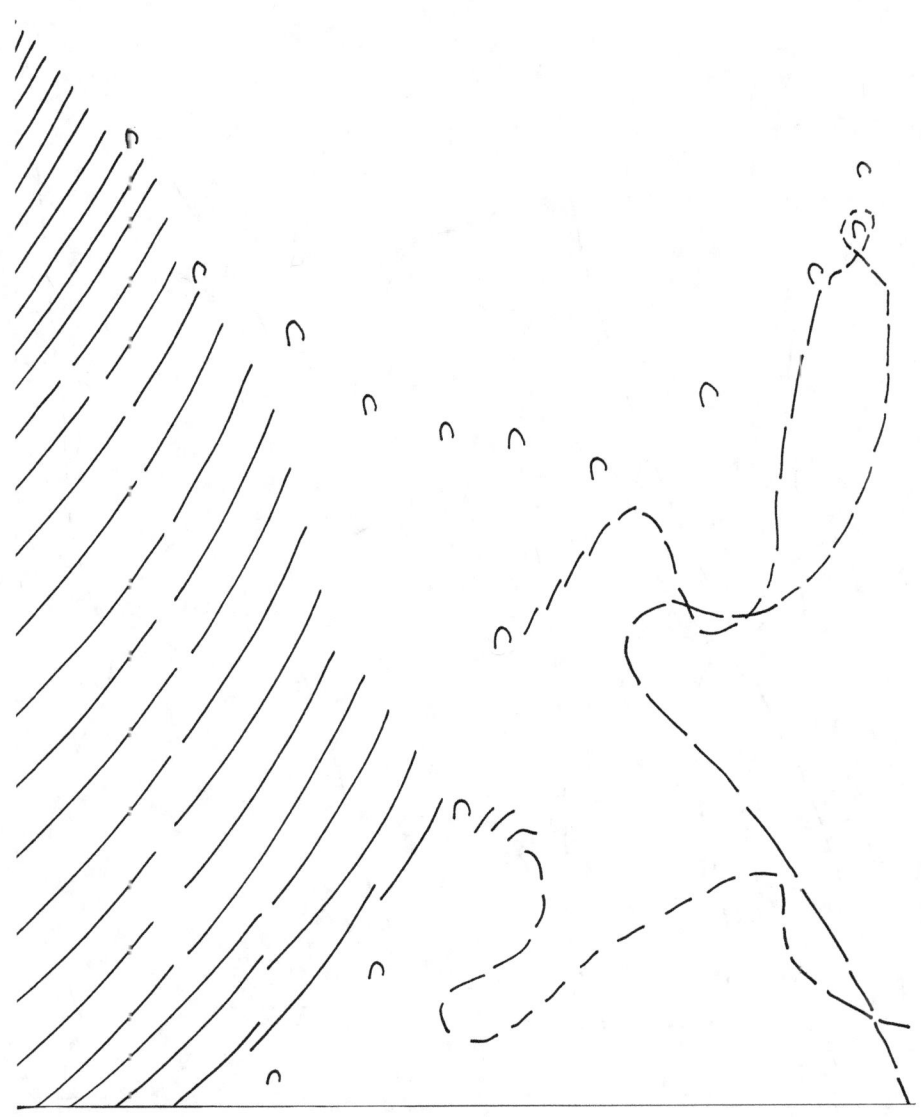

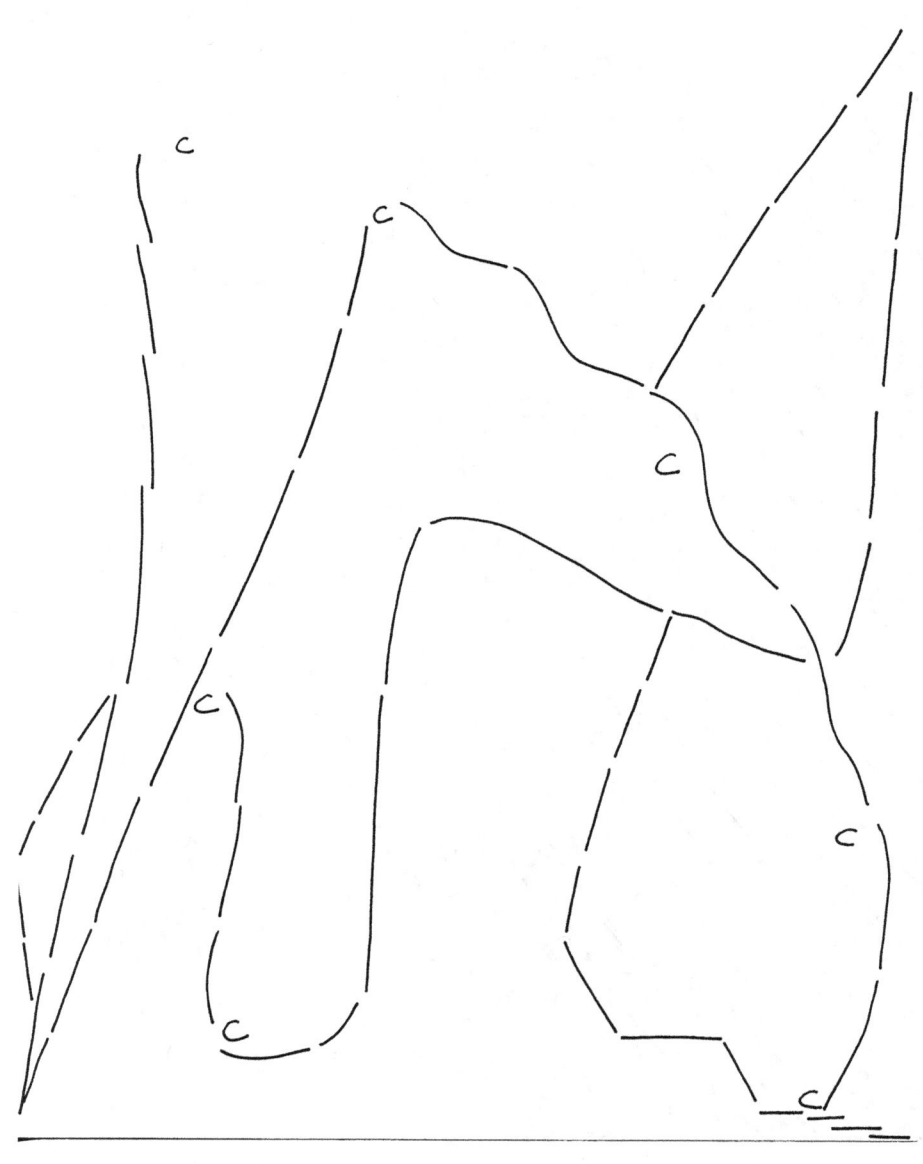

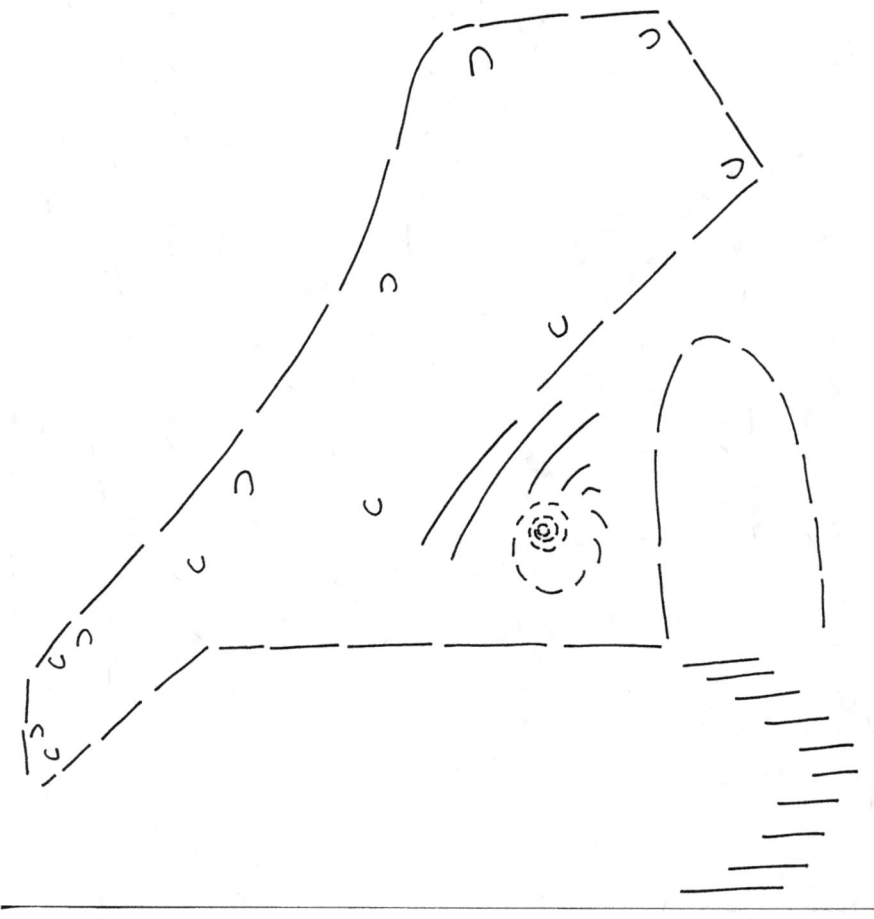

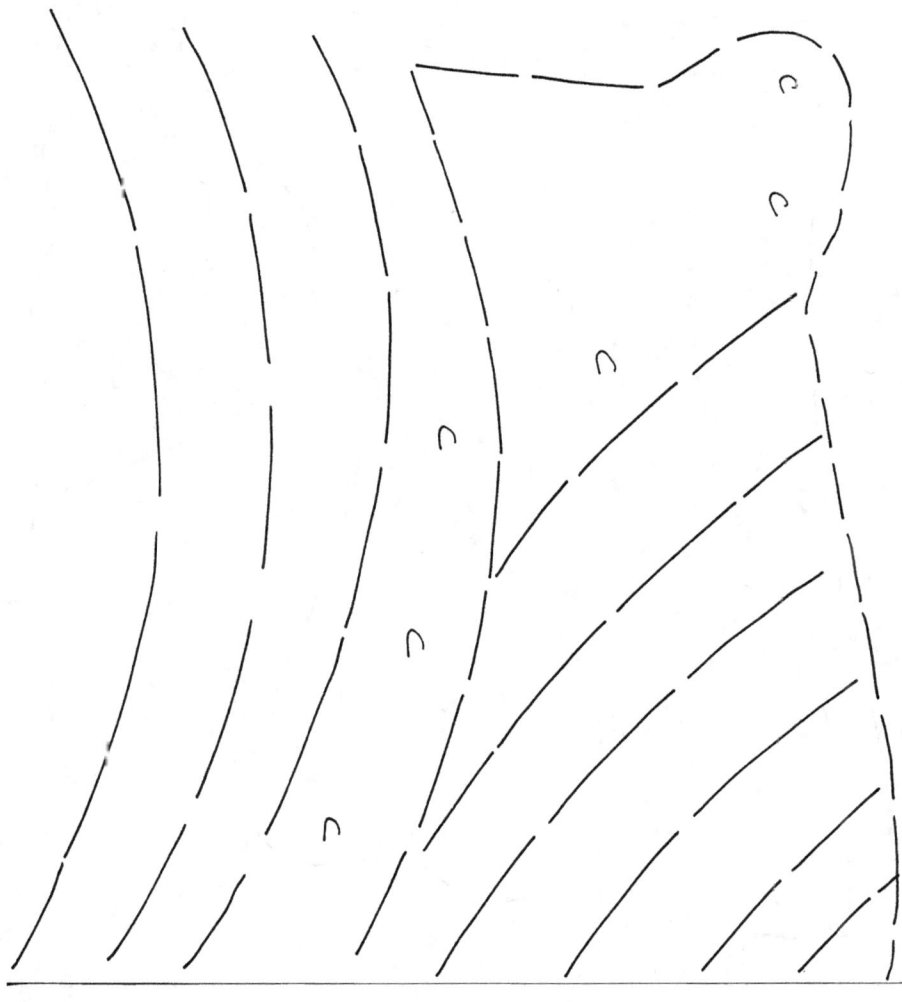

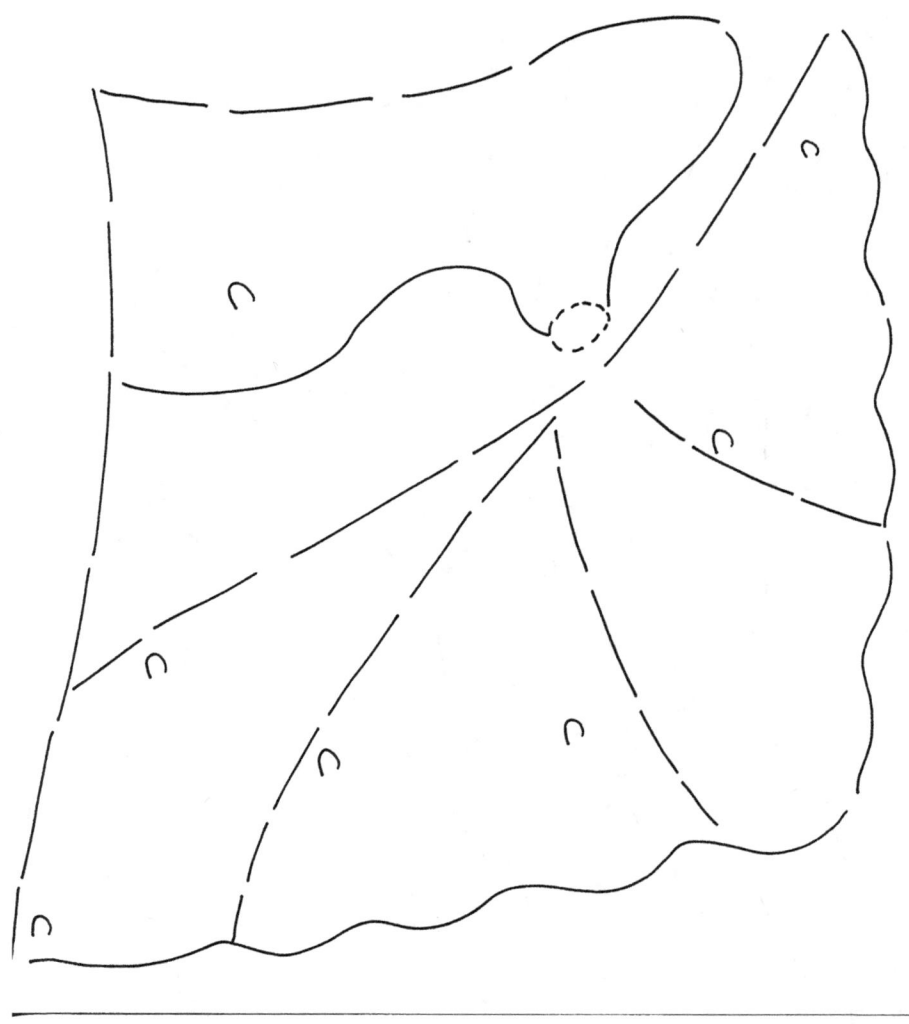

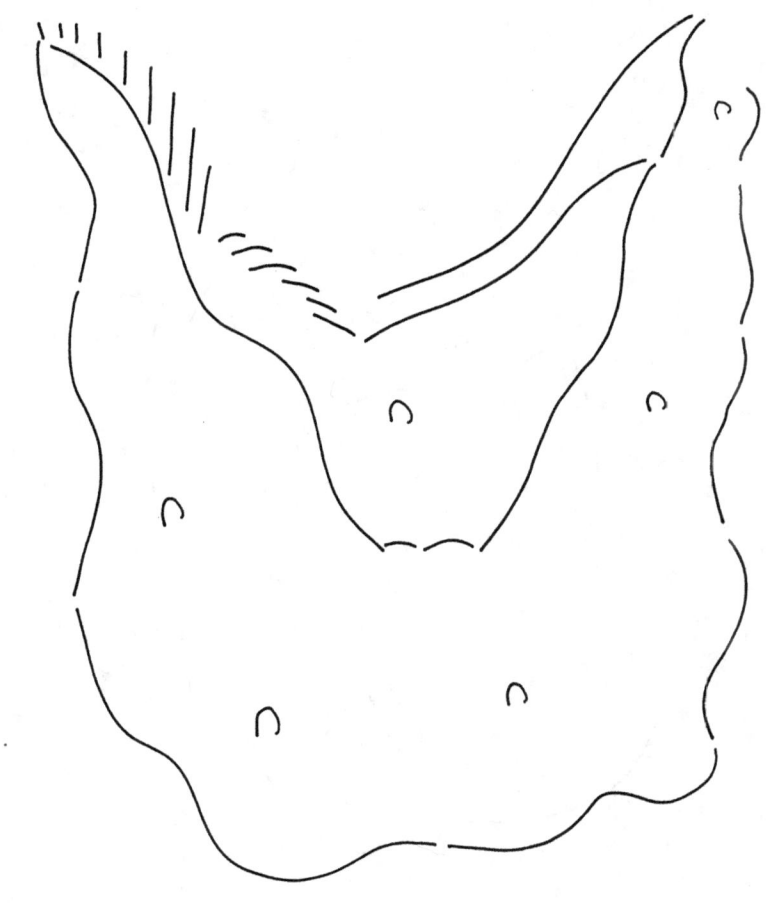

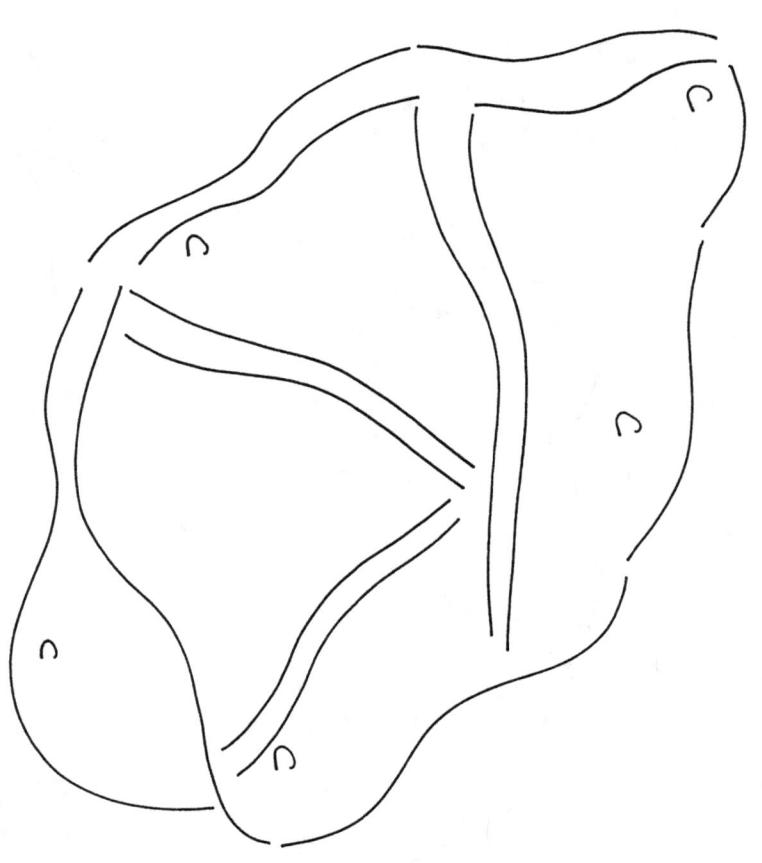

STORIES AND IMAGES FOR THOSE WITH SEVERE DISABILITIES
'Soft' Images

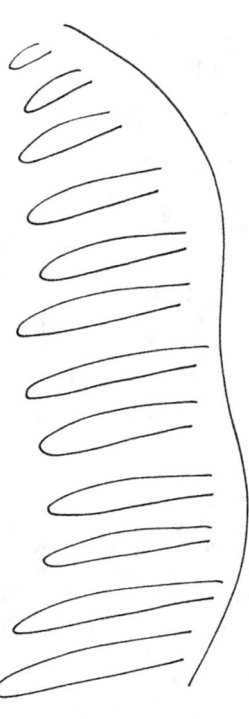

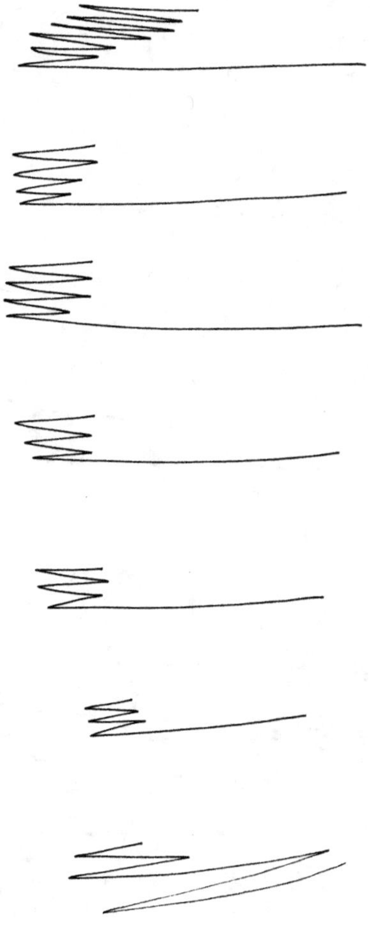

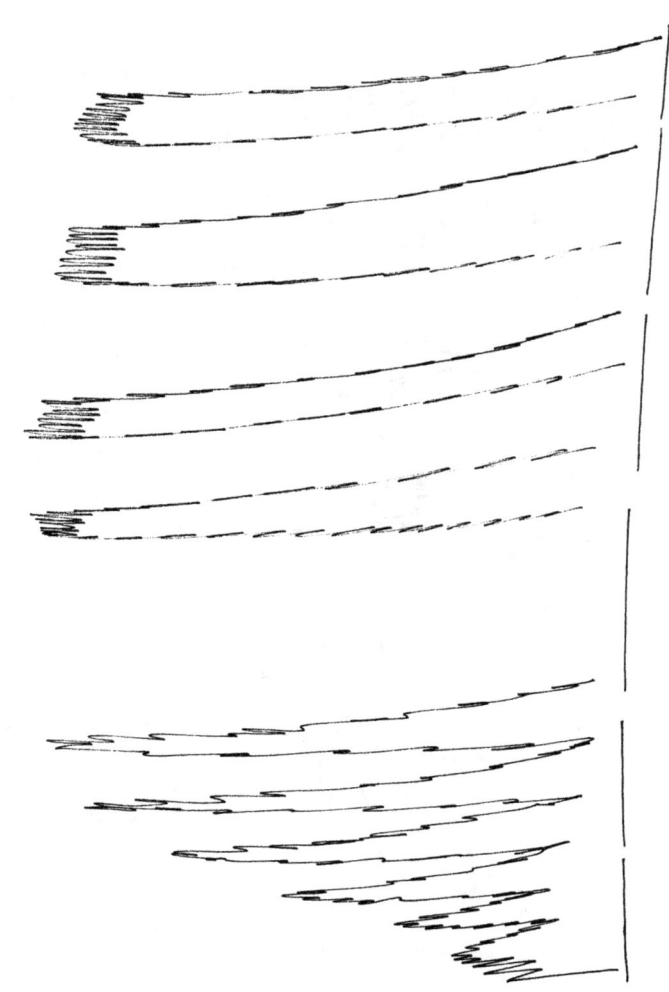

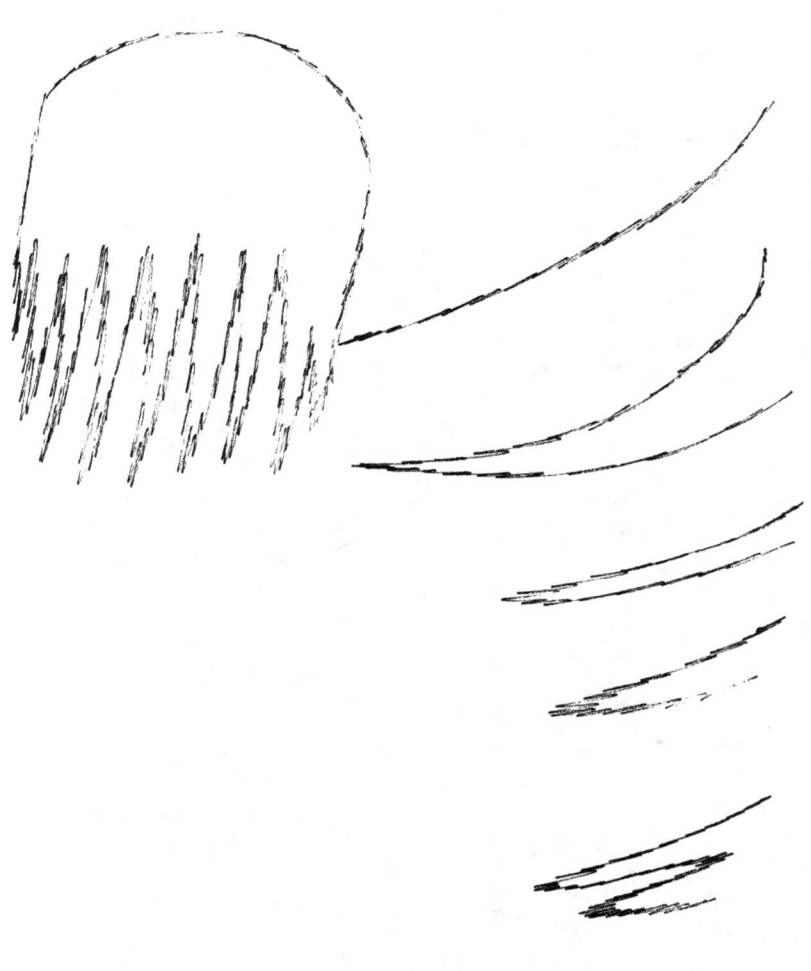

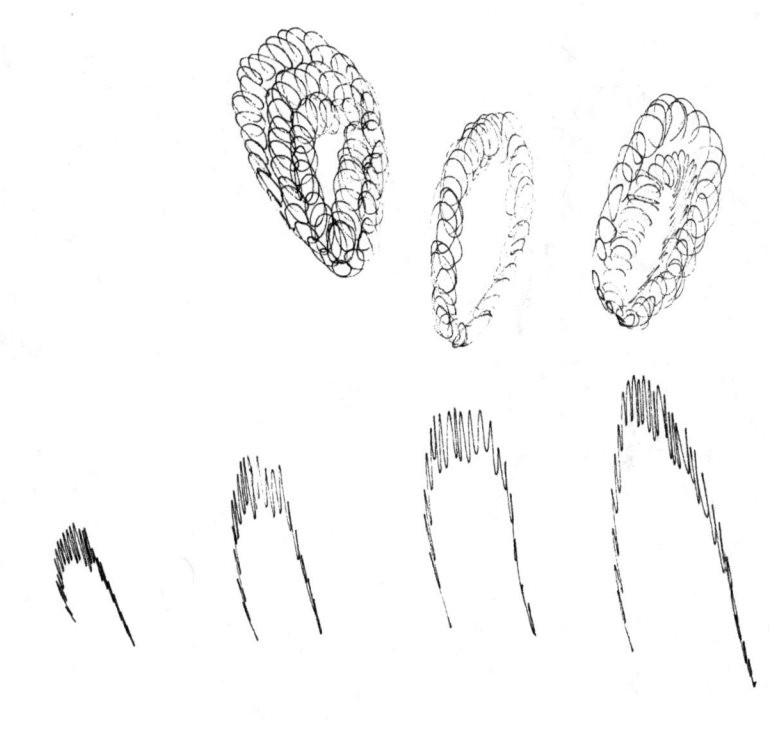

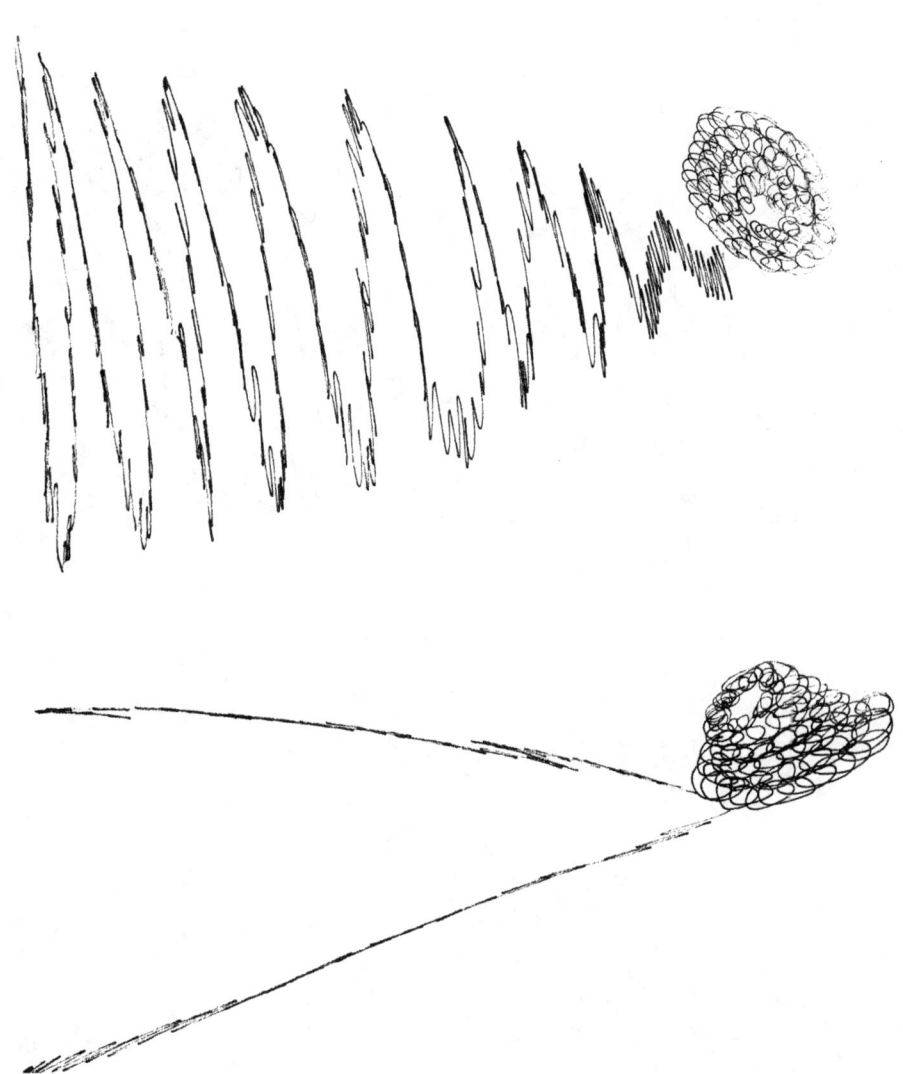

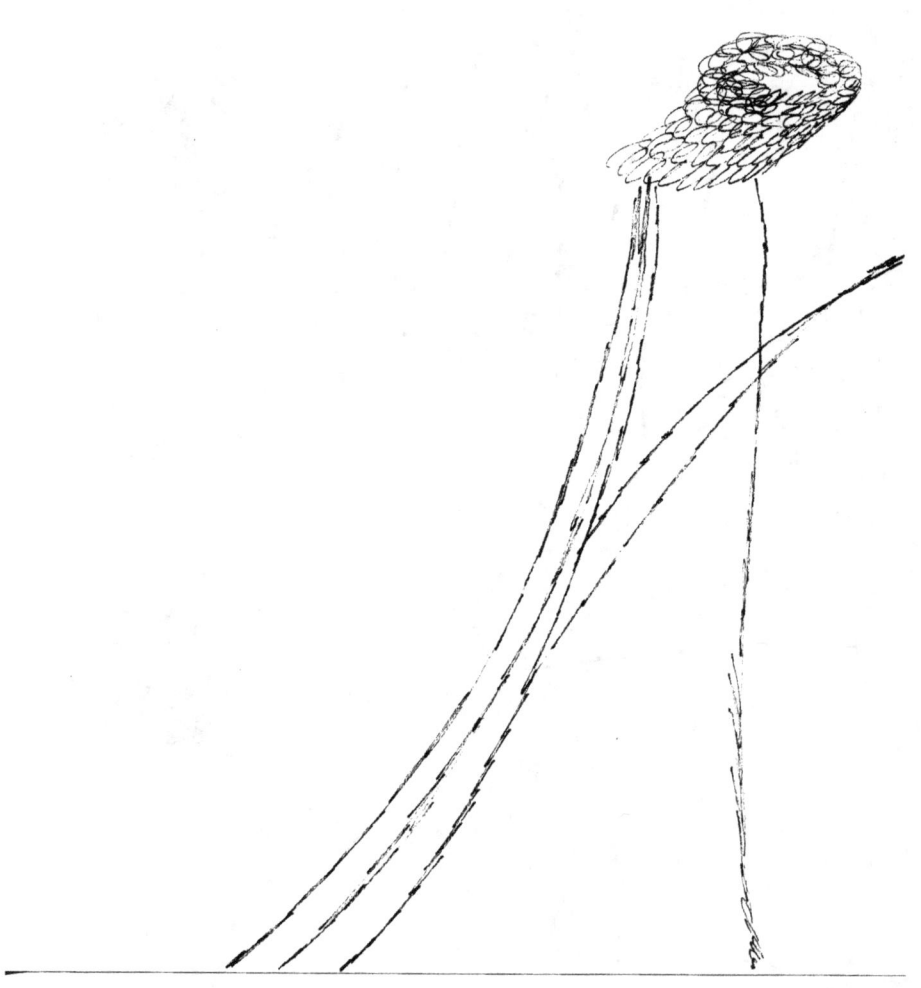

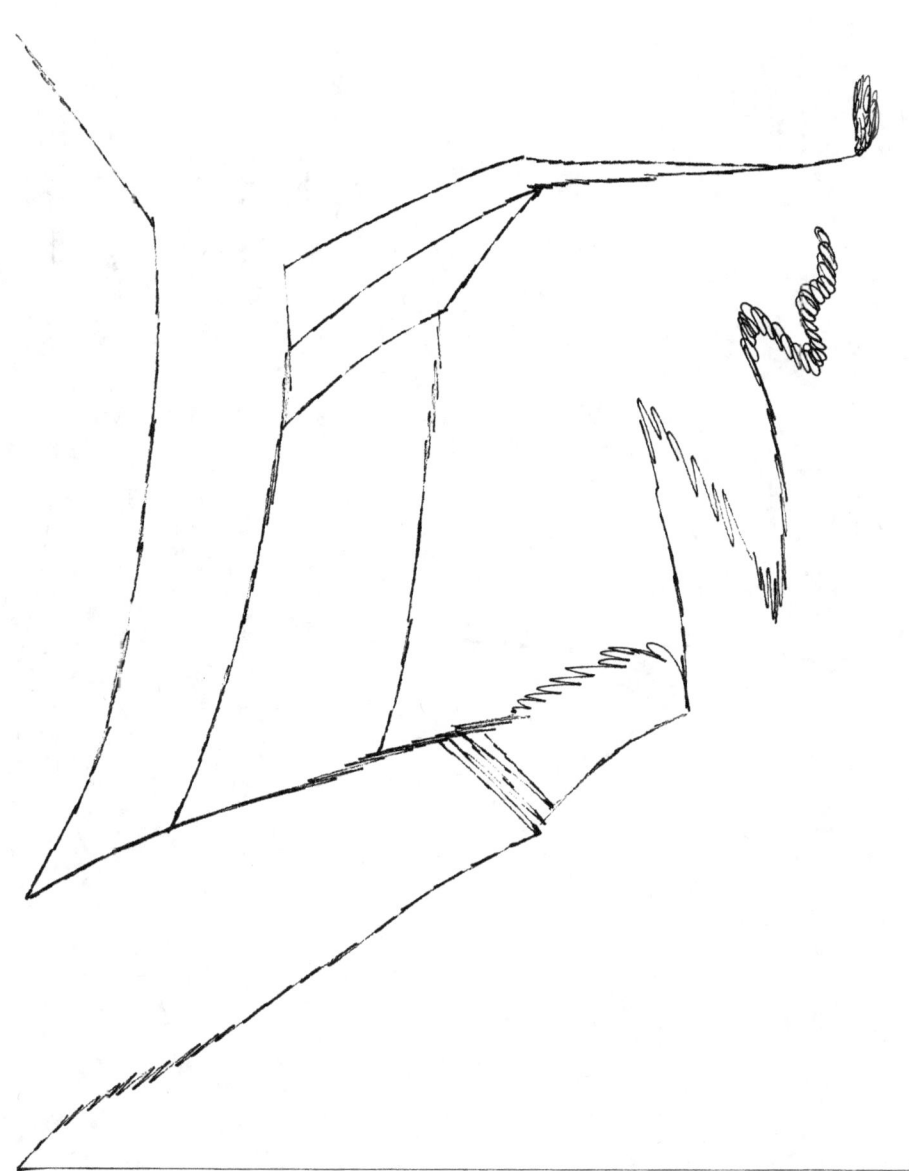

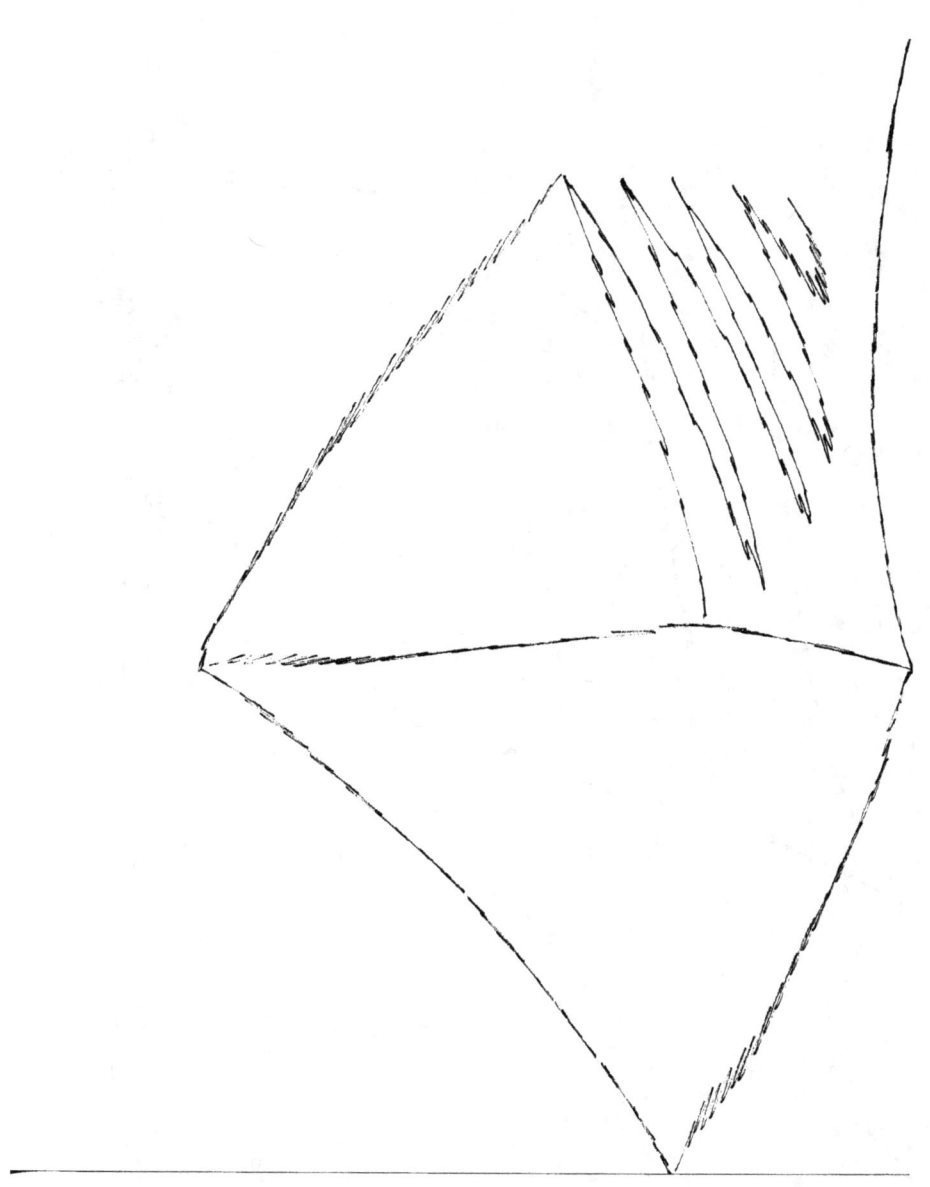

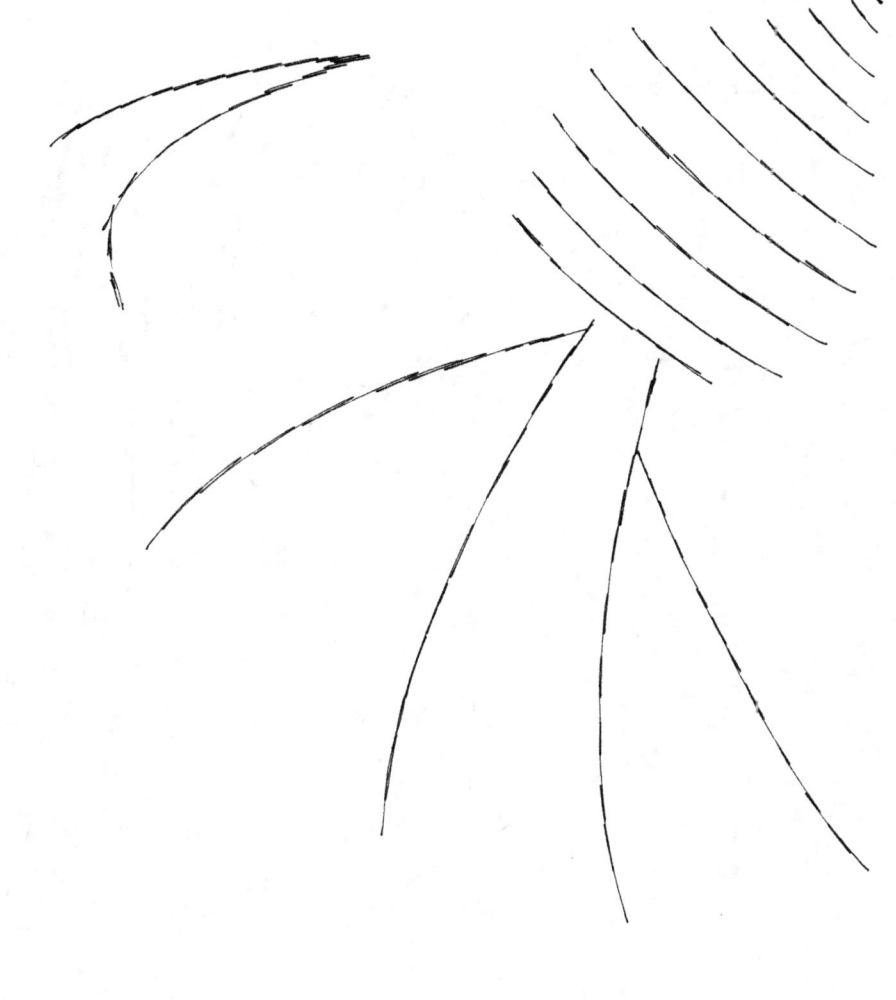

GENTLE 'DOT' IMAGES
A language that
emerges from the brain

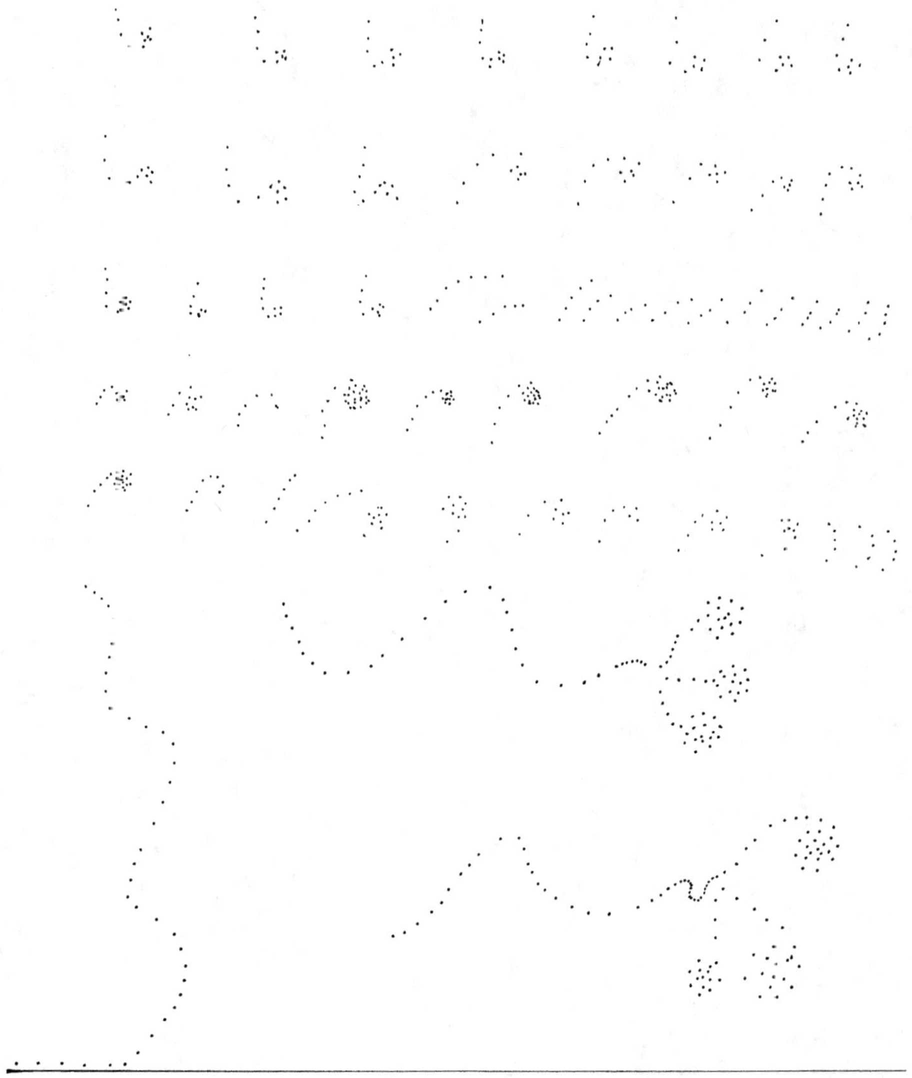

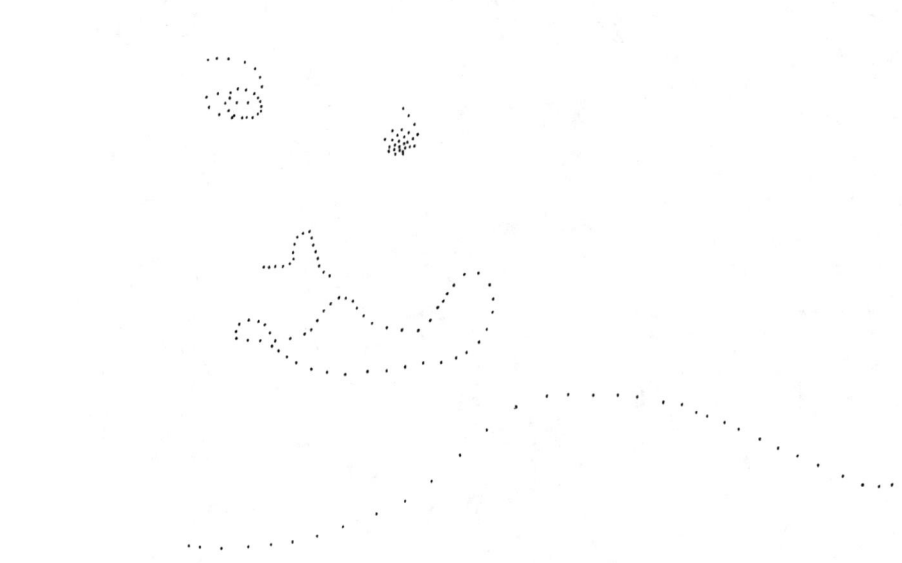

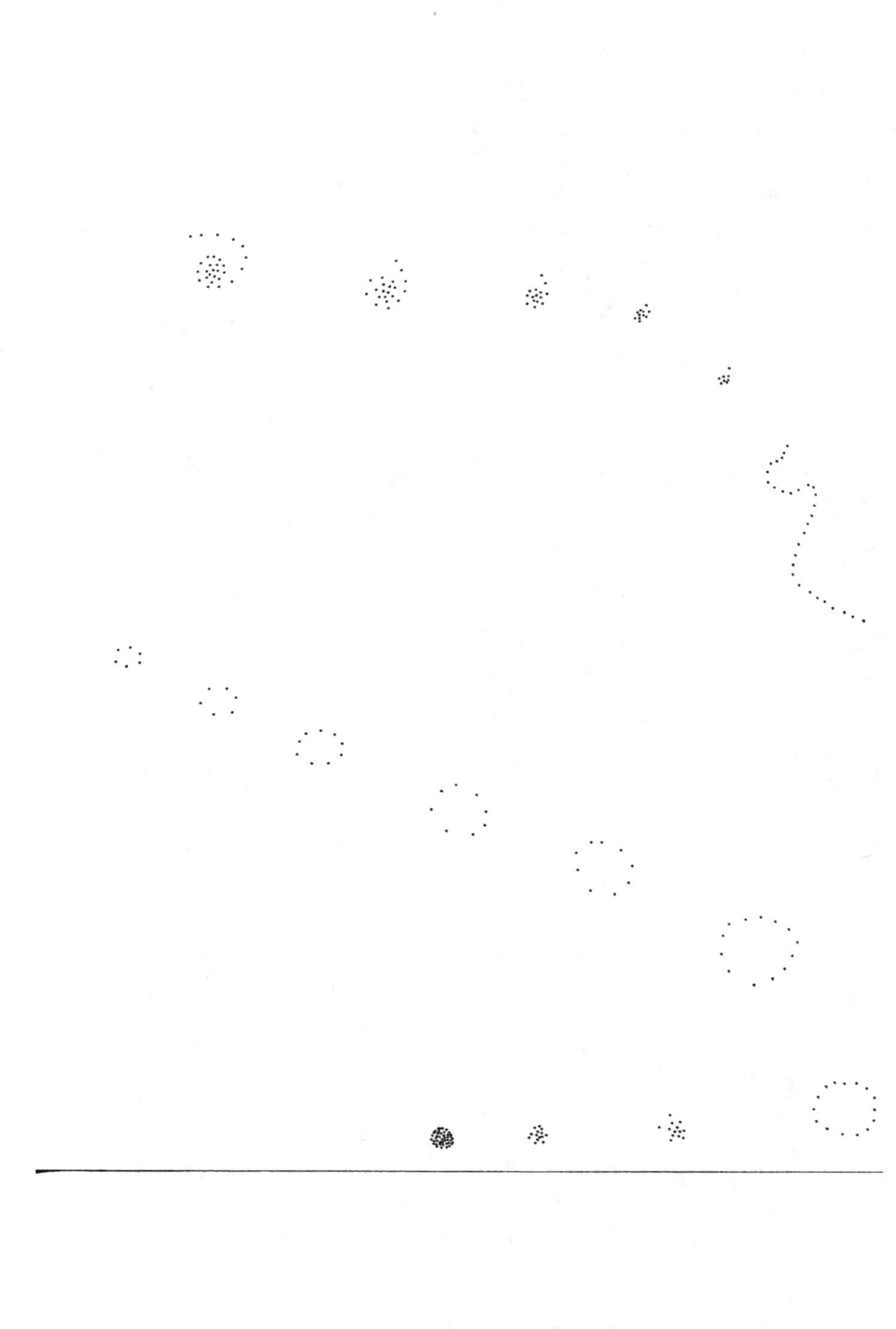

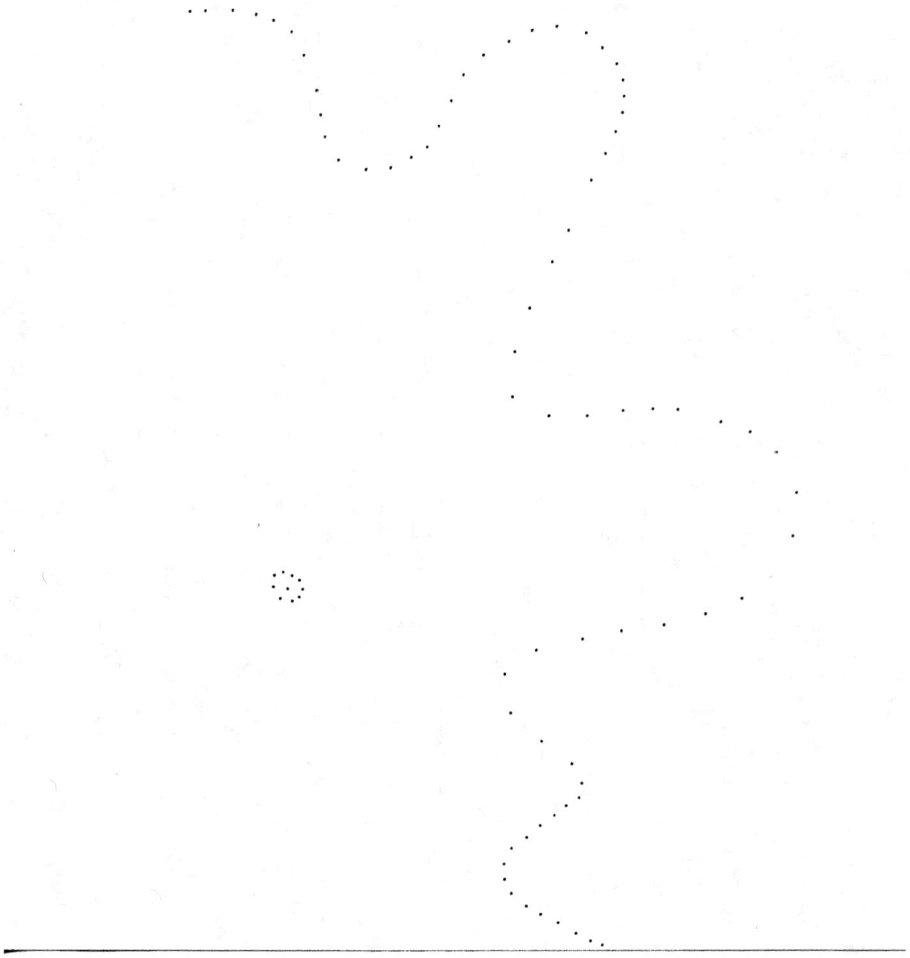

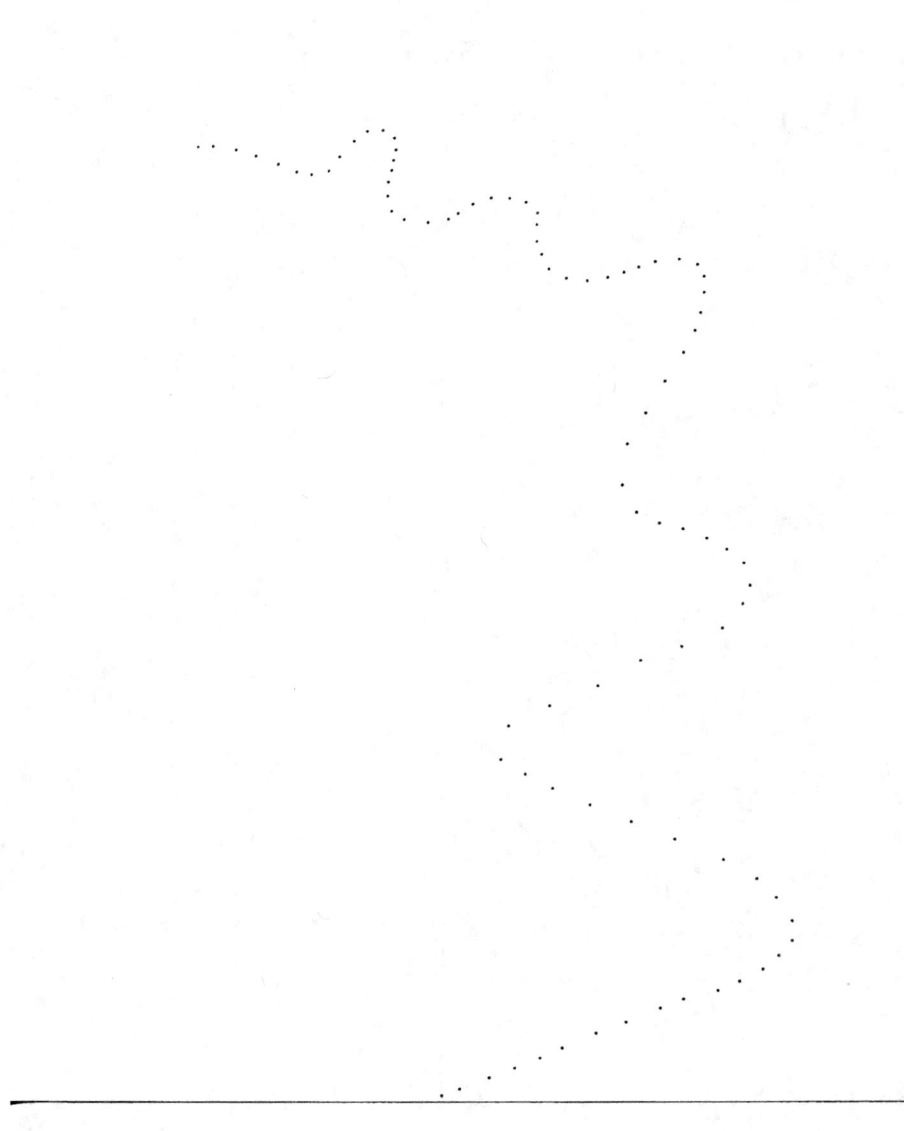

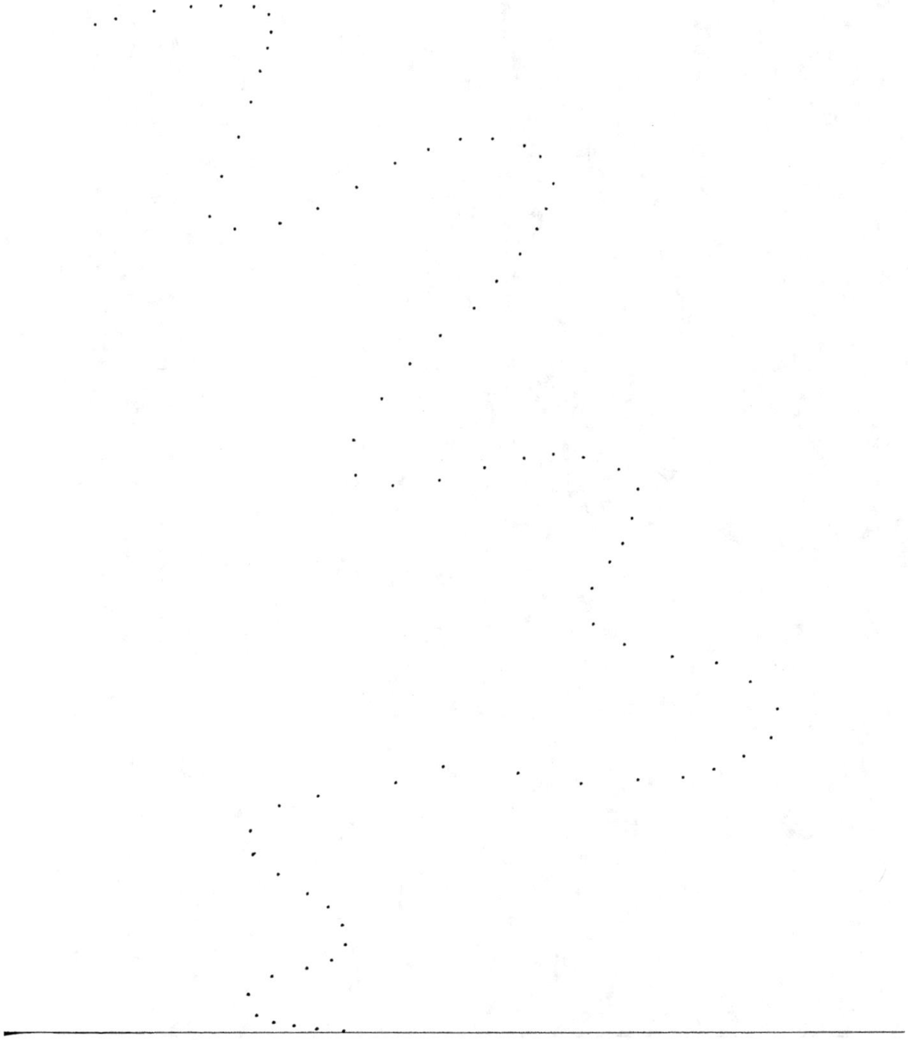

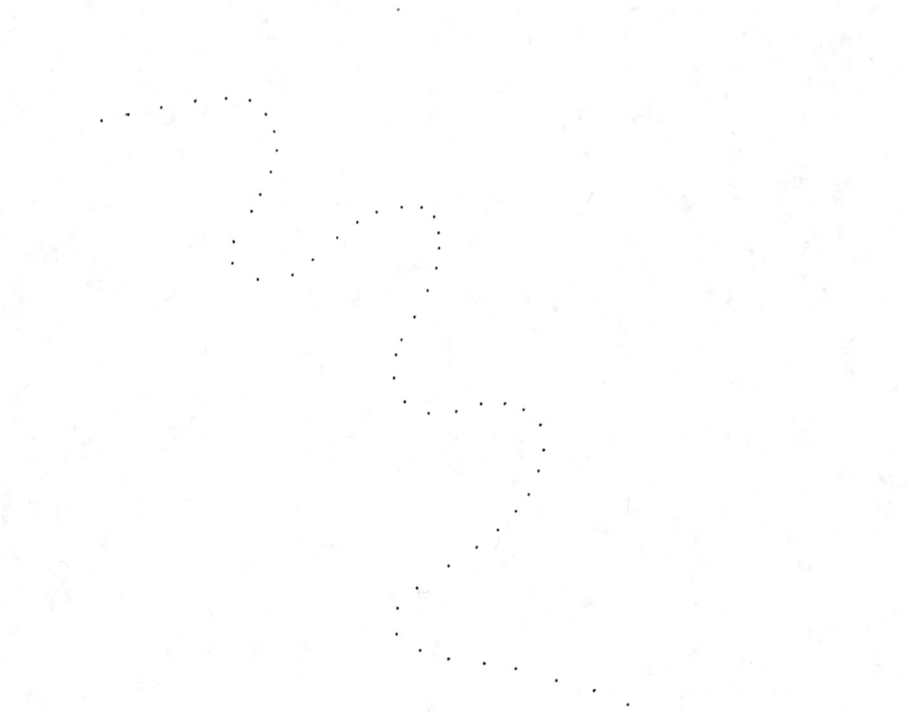

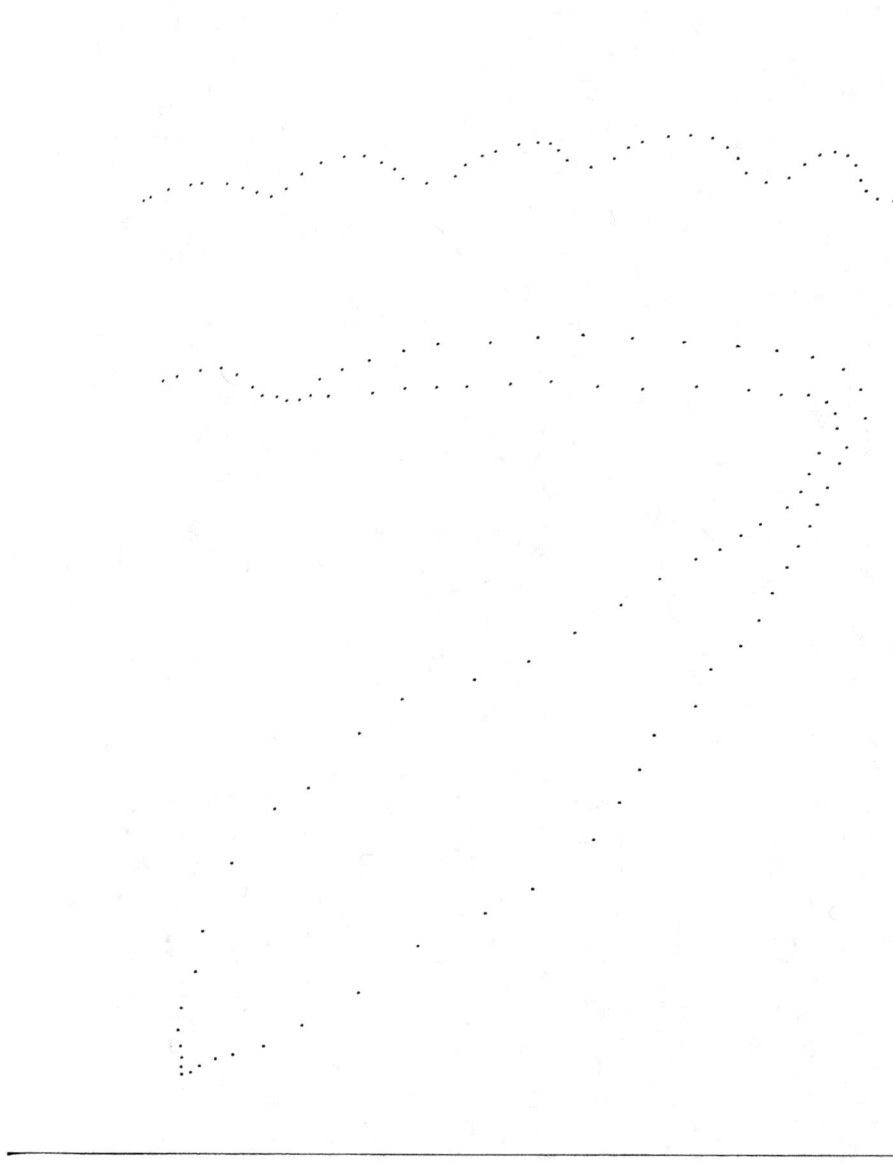

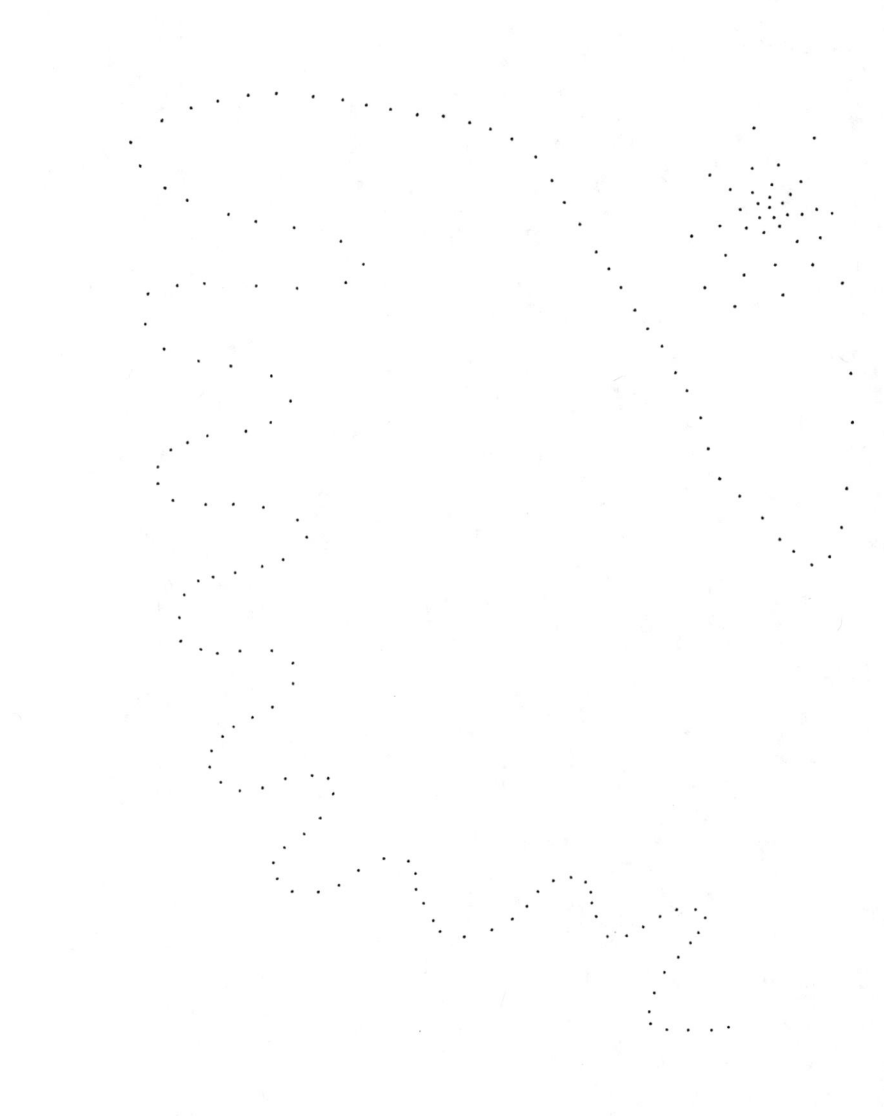

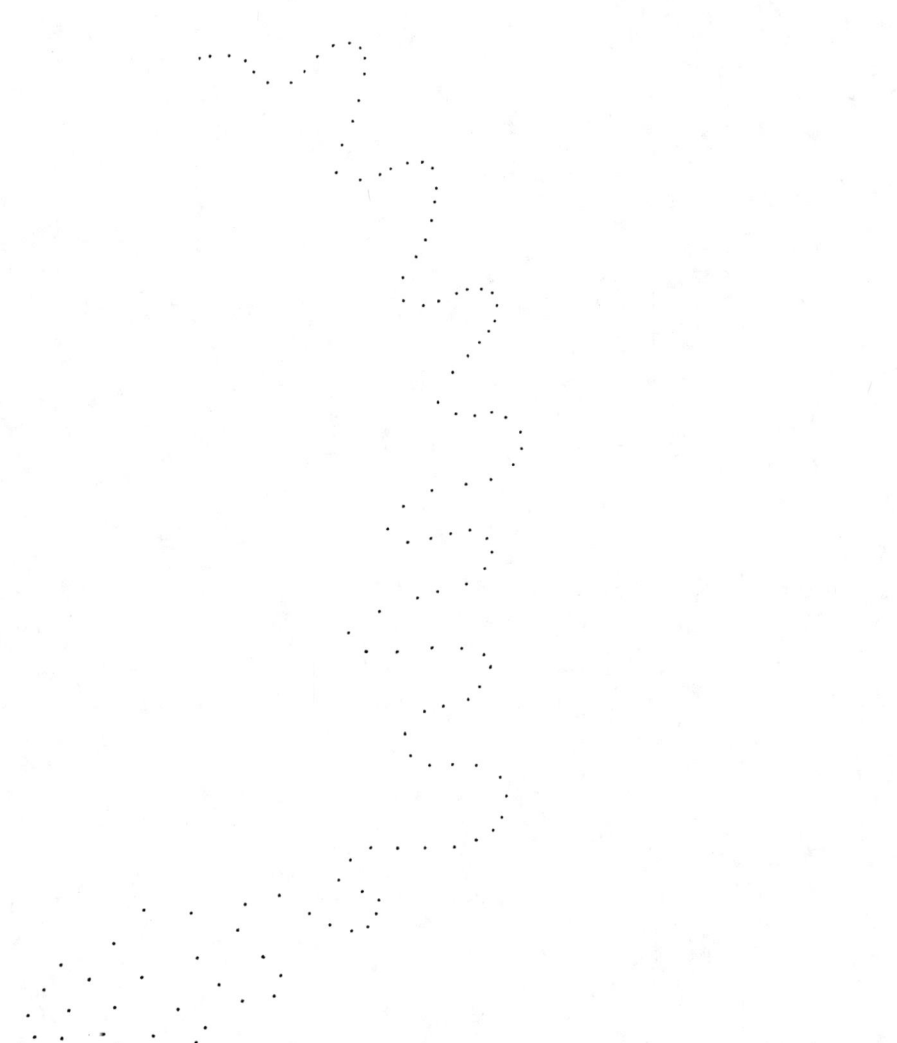

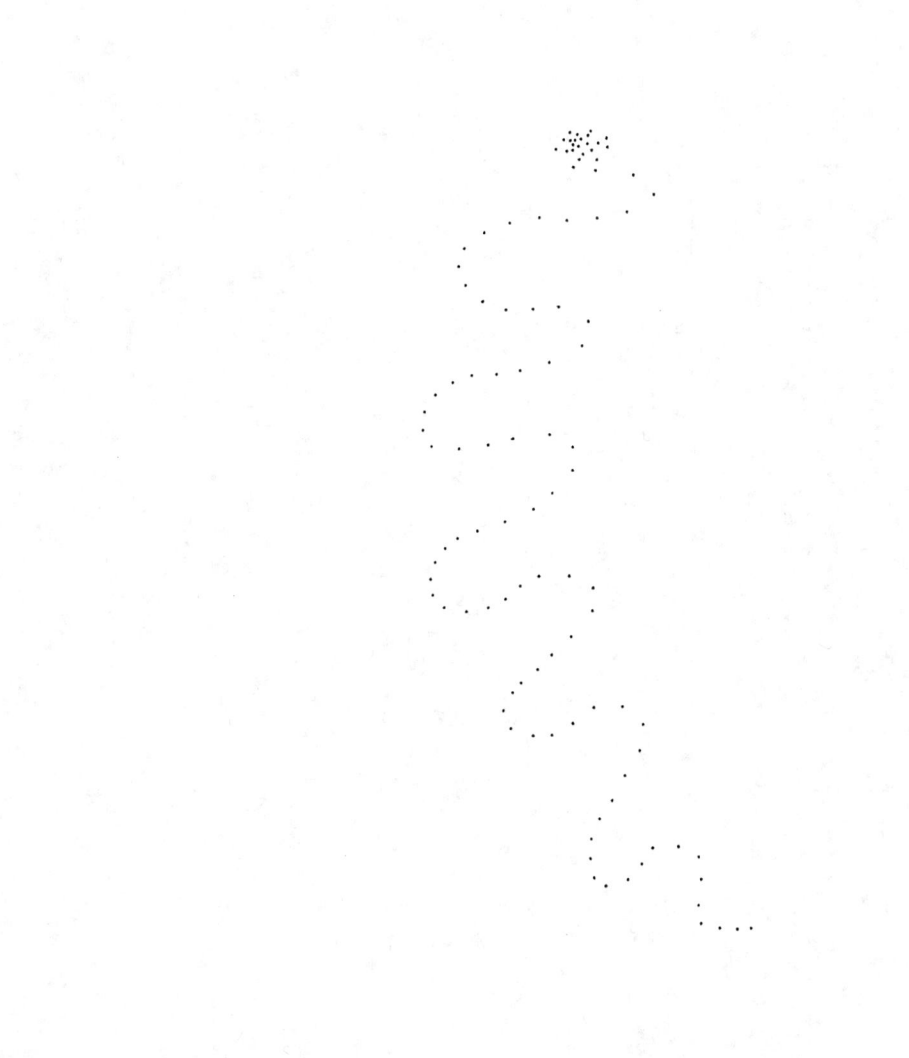

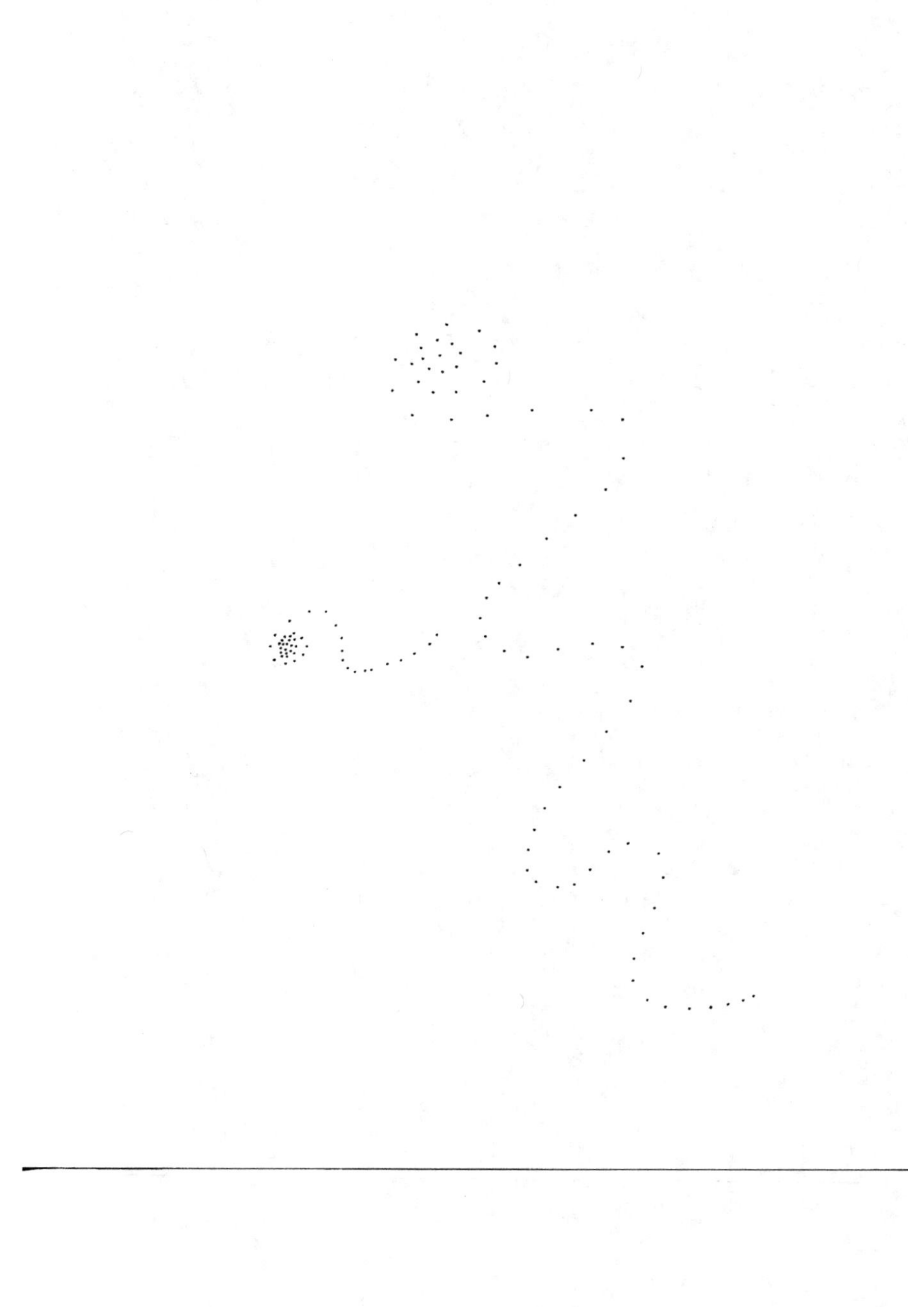

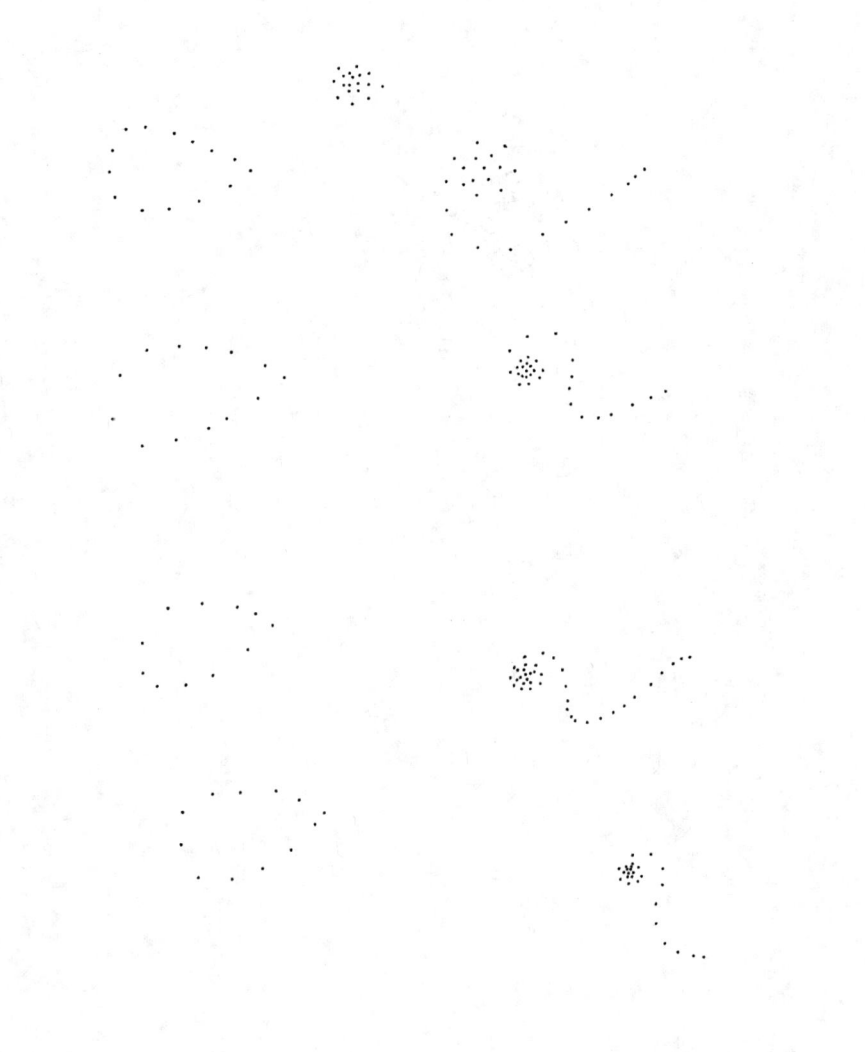

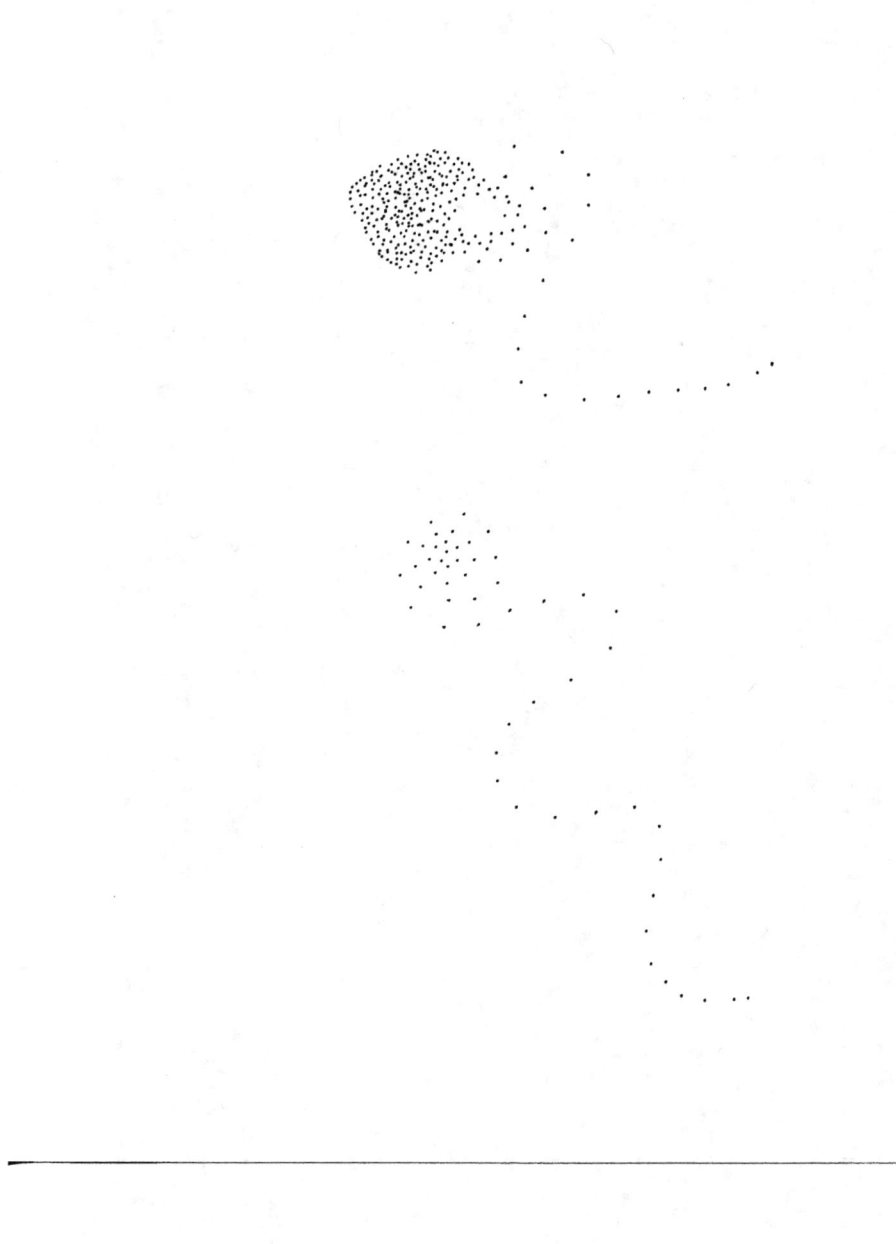

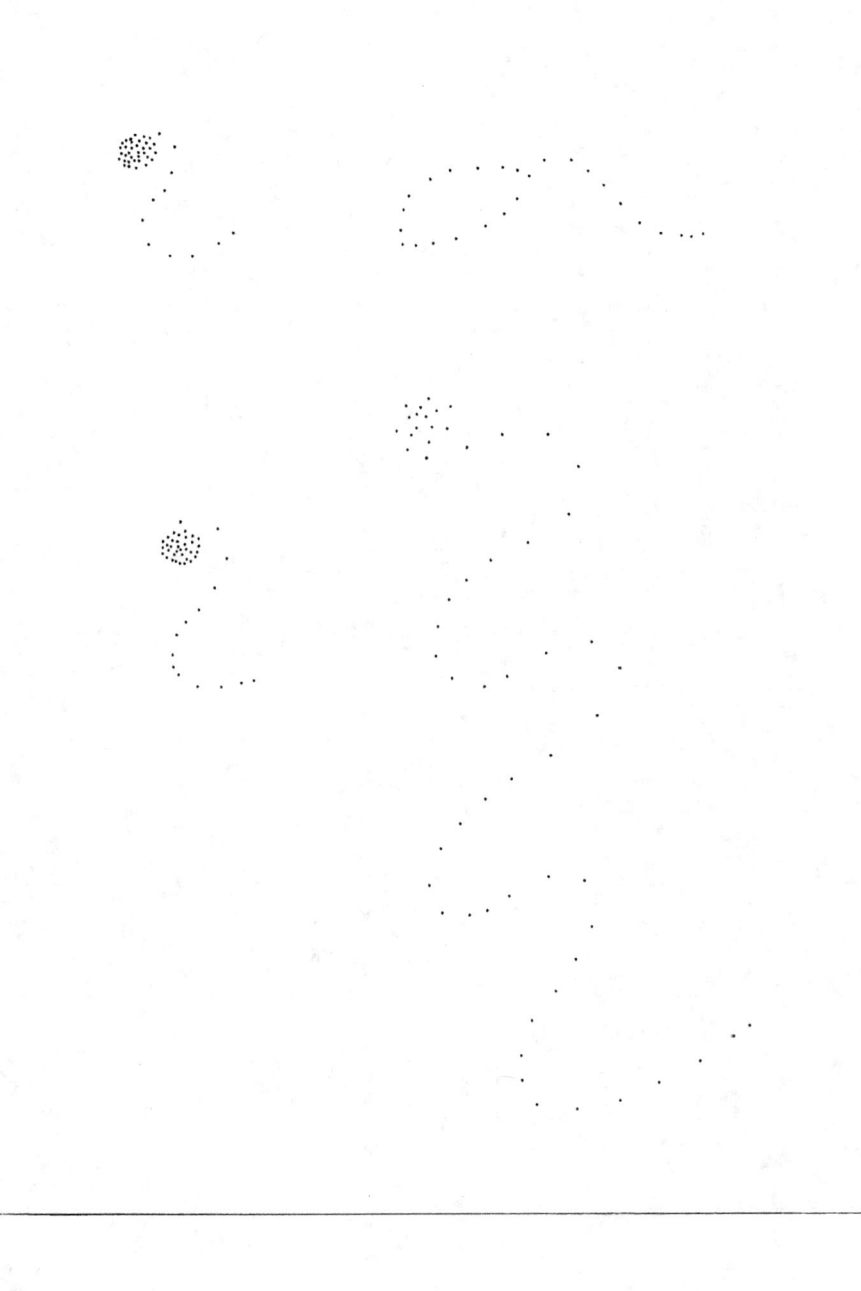

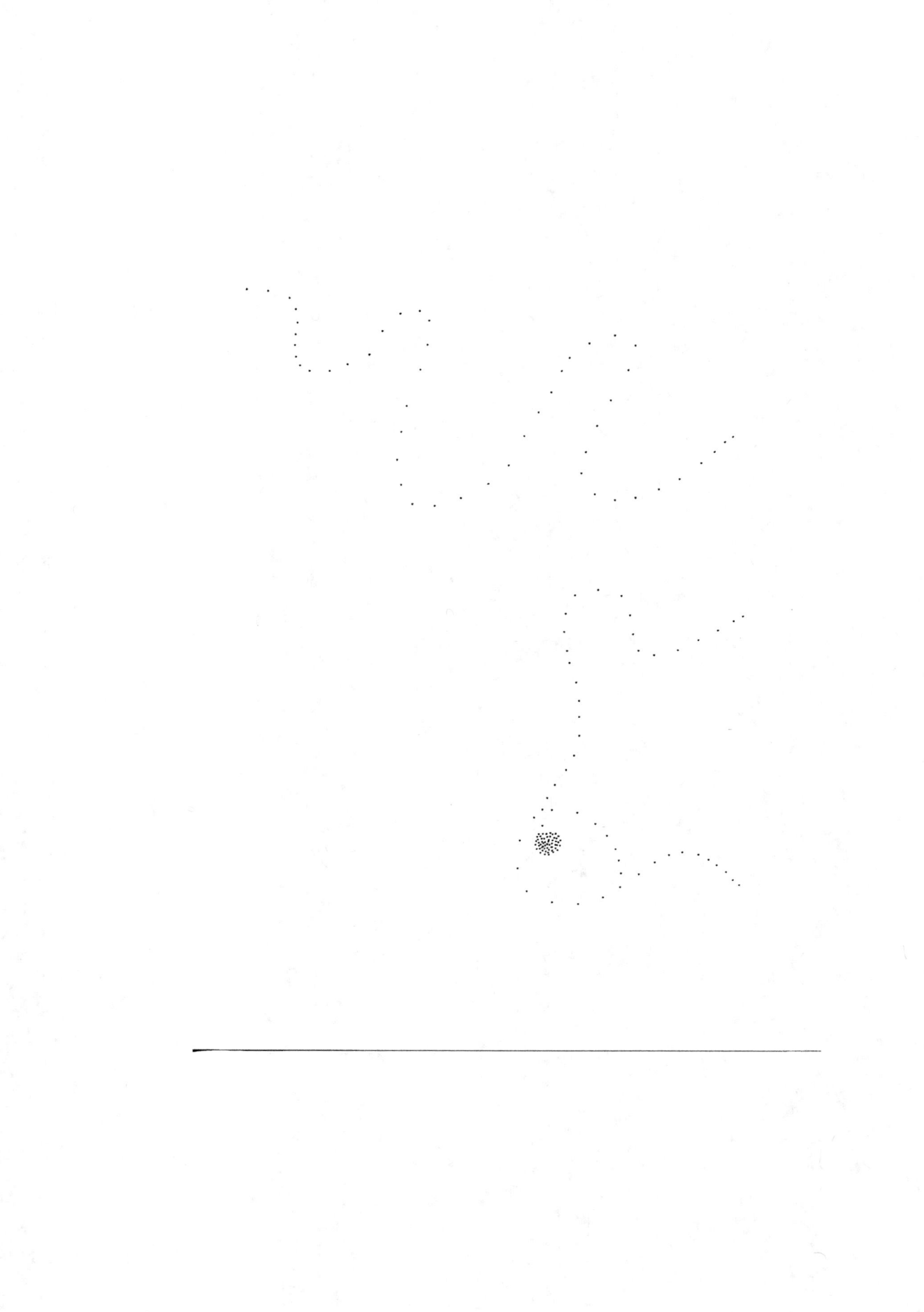

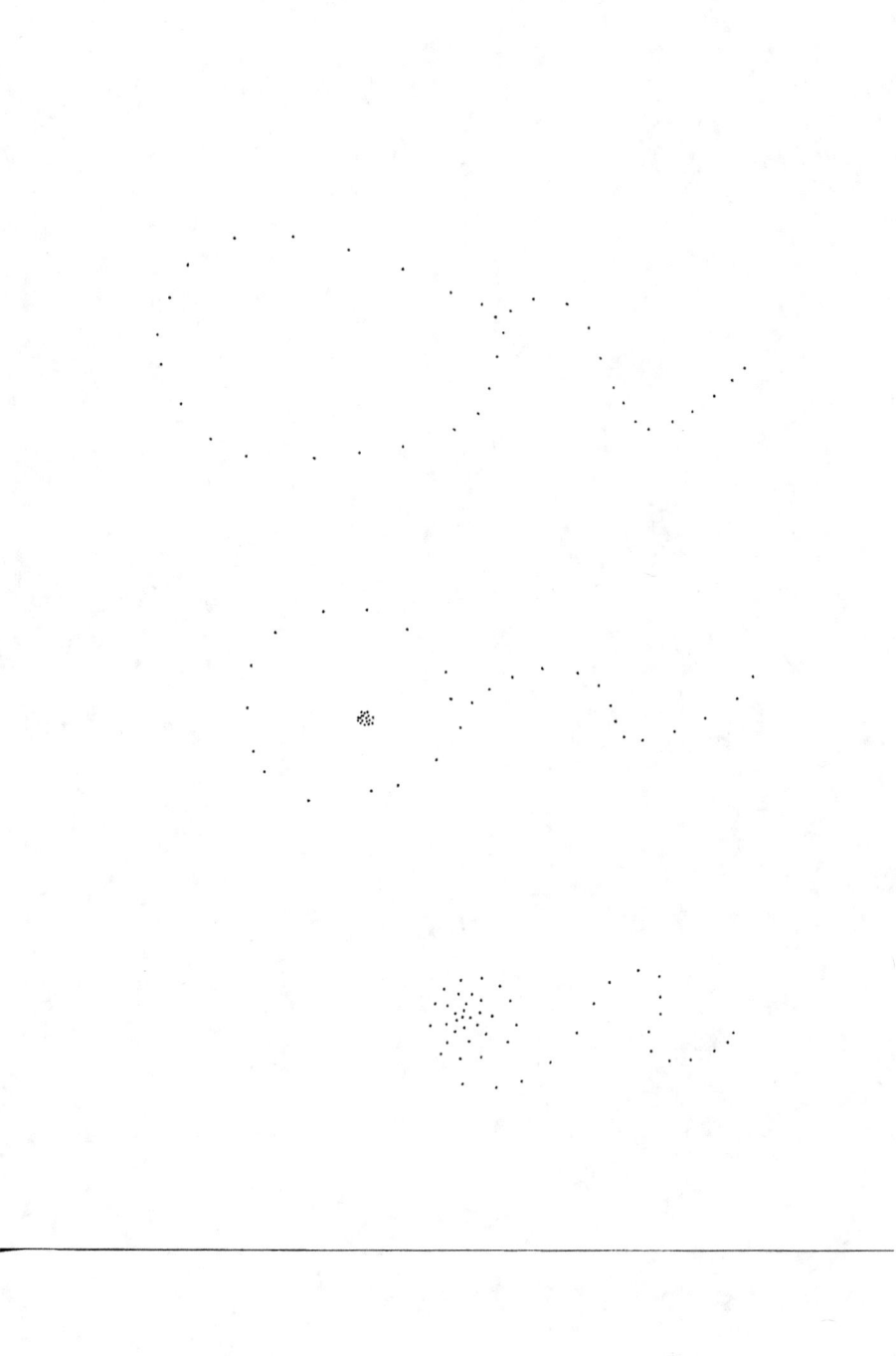

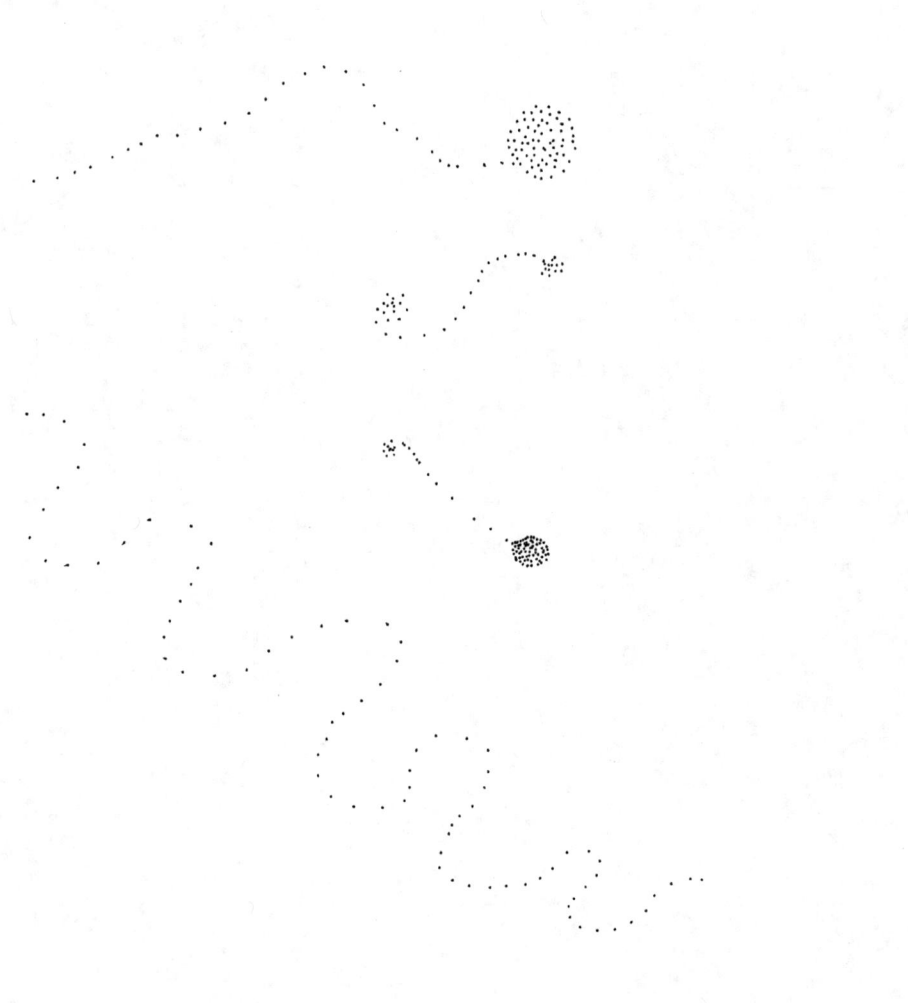

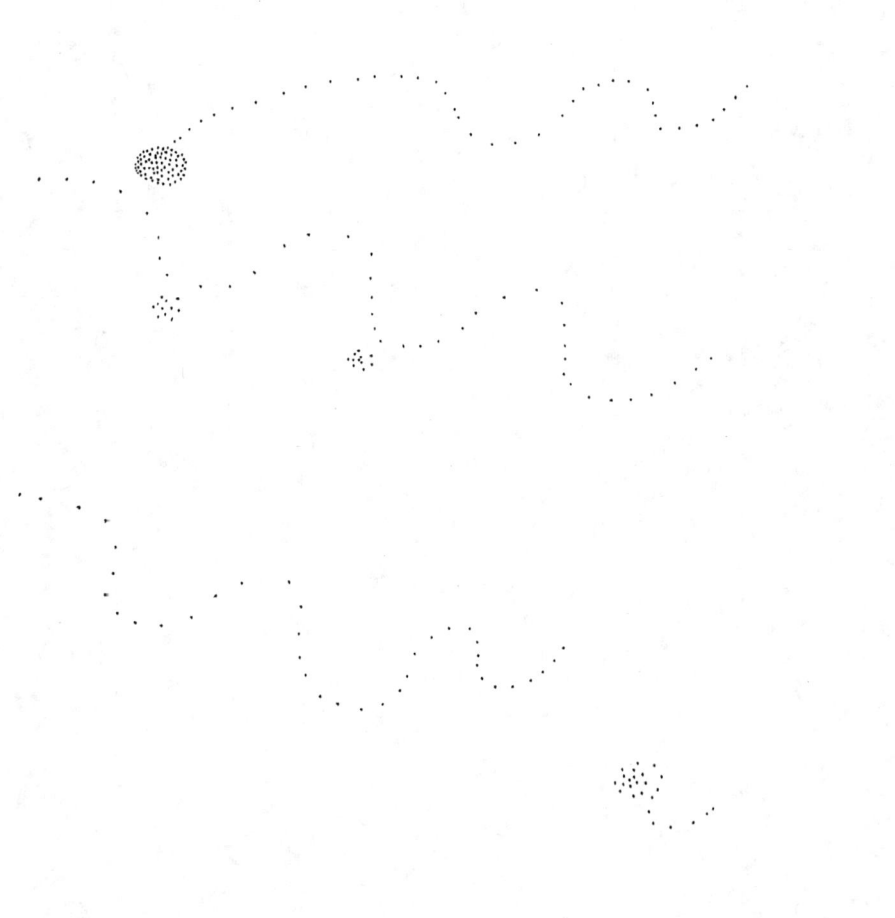

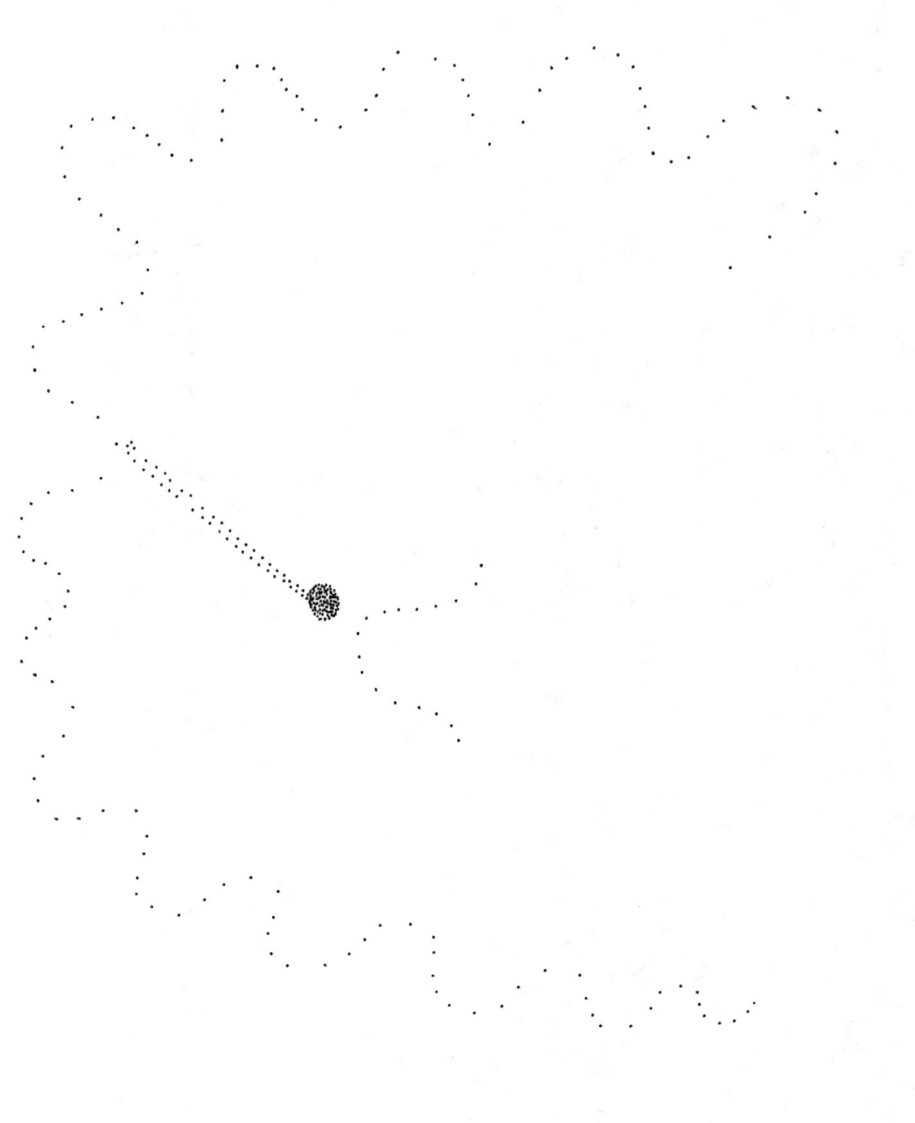

www.ingramcontent.com/pod-product-compliance
Lightning Source LLC
Chambersburg PA
CBHW081356280526
45788CB00009B/2901